Double Fault

My Rise and Fall, and My Road Back

Roscoe Tanner with Mike Yorkey

TRIUMPH
B O O K S
CHICAGO

Library of Congress Cataloging-in-Publication Data

Tanner, Roscoe, 1951–
     Double fault : my rise and fall, and my road back / Roscoe Tanner with Mike Yorkey.
         p. cm.
     Includes index.
     ISBN-13: 978-1-57243-779-1
     ISBN-10: 1-57243-779-0
     1. Tanner, Roscoe, 1951– 2. Tennis players—United States—Biography. I. Yorkey, Mike. II. Title.

GV994.T36A3 2005
796.342'092—dc22
[B]

                                                                    2005041849

This book is available in quantity at special discounts for your group or organization. For further information, contact:

Triumph Books
542 South Dearborn Street
Suite 750
Chicago, Illinois 60605
(312) 939-3330
Fax (312) 663-3557

Printed in U.S.A.
ISBN-13: 978-1-57243-779-1
ISBN-10: 1-57243-779-0
Design by Patricia Frey
All photos courtesy of the Tanner family except where indicated otherwise.

To Mom

You were always there for me.

Contents

Foreword

Back in the late eighties, I got involved in designing a tennis facility for the Sherwood Country Club, an exclusive, upscale development near Westlake Village in Southern California.

I've seen some high-end clubs in my day, but Sherwood Country Club ranked near the top. The development company asked for my advice on building an elegant country-manor clubhouse that would front 14 courts comprising three surfaces: hard-court, grass, and clay. For once, tennis players would be pampered like golfers.

I flew out to Los Angeles several times to meet with the developers. At one gathering, I was asked who they should hire to be the director of tennis.

I thought for a moment, and then the answer came to me. "Roscoe Tanner," I replied.

I believed Roscoe would be a great fit for the Sherwood Country Club, but I harbored an ulterior motive as well: I had heard rumors that Roscoe had fallen on hard times. Maybe running the tennis program at Sherwood Country Club would help turn things around for my former foe.

I wanted to help because I had liked Roscoe ever since our paths crossed on the tennis court. One of the first times we squared off was during an exhibition on the Stanford University courts back in early 1971. Roscoe, one of the top collegiate players in the country, was in his sophomore year at Stanford. As for me, I was 24 years old and among the top 10 players in the world.

In 1971, however, I belonged to the U.S. Army—Uncle Sam had drafted me for the Vietnam War. I was stationed at Fort Ord on the Northern California coast, about an hour's drive from Stanford. Part of my responsibilities was representing the U.S. Army as a tennis player and member of the U.S. Davis Cup team, which was good PR for the U.S. military.

Dick Gould, the Stanford tennis coach, approached me about playing in a fund-raising exhibition event for the team. I was certainly willing to help out, so coach Gould pitted Roscoe against me in the featured singles match. I don't remember who won, but I sure remember facing that famous serve of his. He whistled more than a few deliveries by me that day.

When Roscoe joined the pro ranks, no one ever called him a "bad boy" or "Superbrat." Compared to John McEnroe, Jimmy Connors, or Ilie Nastase, Roscoe was a Boy Scout in tennis whites, a straight arrow who thanked the ballboys and little old ladies who volunteered at our tournaments.

But as you'll learn in *Double Fault*, when Roscoe's wife, Nancy, stopped traveling with him, Roscoe succumbed to the temptations available to rich and famous athletes. My wife, Margie, and I could see that Roscoe was not in a good situation, so it came as no surprise to us when his marriage ended in divorce toward the end of his career.

For the next decade or so, his life fell into a sinkhole of financial disasters and personal destruction—a series of double faults and missed opportunities. That's why I helped Roscoe get that head pro position at Sherwood Country Club, thinking that a steady, well-paying job would land him back on his feet.

Then I heard bits and pieces of some odd things happening to him during the late nineties and into the new millennium. Apparently, he owed some guy in Florida a lot of money for a boat, and a New Jersey woman claimed that Roscoe was the father of her daughter.

Meanwhile, I continued to run into Roscoe periodically, like the time at the 2002 Wimbledon championships, where my old doubles partner, Bob Lutz, and I played him and Australian legend John Newcombe in the Gentlemen's 45 and Older doubles event.

The Wimbledon committee put our match on Centre Court at the end of the middle Monday, which was quite an honor. As far as I was concerned, that famous serve still had some heat on it, and Roscoe seemed to be in the best shape of all of us. Bob and I managed, however, to win a three-setter as long shadows settled over the court.

After the match, Roscoe told me that he had been living in Europe for more than a year. He had been coaching a young British player, but that hadn't worked out as he had hoped, so he had moved on to coaching jobs in France and Switzerland. Those opportunities hadn't panned out either. Now he was living in Germany, he said, optimistic that life would get better teaching at a German club. I wished him all the best.

That's why it came as a shock when I heard in the summer of 2003 that Roscoe had been picked up and jailed in Germany. Then he was extradited to Florida and subsequently imprisoned in New Jersey. Every time I saw prisoners on TV wearing orange jumpsuits, I tried to picture Roscoe in that situation, which was difficult to do. I had never heard of a *tennis player* going to jail, but that's exactly what happened to Roscoe.

I found out Roscoe's address while he was imprisoned in New Jersey, and I wrote him a note of encouragement. I think Roscoe appreciated that I had not forgotten him, and we began talking on the phone. Since his release, I've tried to be there for Roscoe, to give him a hand up as he rebuilds his life.

That's why I'm pleased to introduce *Double Fault*. What you're about to read is a brutally honest account of a celebrity athlete who experienced the riches of the world—only to see everything evaporate in his hands. In this spellbinding book, Roscoe accounts for the behavior that led to two divorces, fathering a daughter out of wedlock, and writing a bad check that led to a 10-month imprisonment from June 18, 2003, to April 19, 2004. I'm confident that this powerful story of a prodigal in tennis shorts will move you deeply.

Ready to get started? Good, because I just heard the chair umpire say, "Tanner to serve."

—Stan Smith

Acknowledgments

At the risk of forgetting or excluding someone, I would like to thank some people who've had an incredible impact on my life or have been there when I needed a hand up.

For my family: my father, Leonard Roscoe; my wife, Margaret; and my sister, Sherry Earnhart.

From my tennis days: Dick Gould, Chico Hagey, Bobby Kreiss, and Lorne Kuhle.

For protecting me in the Florida jail: Ron Ware and Gregory "J. J." Moore.

For help in my faith: Stan Smith, Jim Hiskey, Jim Stump, Doug Coe, Tim Timmons, and Milt Richards.

For being special friends: John Devlin and Tom and Marlene Holland.

And finally for my writing partner, Mike Yorkey, who took a chance and wrote my story long before we found Triumph Books to publish it.

1

In Hot Water

June 18, 2003, Ettlingen, Germany, 8:33 A.M.

I lay back in the bathtub, closed my eyes, and allowed the piping-hot water to rejuvenate my sore muscles. At 51 years of age, a hot bath was a welcome tonic to the hours I was putting in on the tennis court. I was teaching 20 to 30 hours a week, batting balls back and forth with an assortment of housewives, lawyers, and hotshot juniors while giving them tips in my kindergarten-level German.

On weekends, I fired up my old serve in age-group tournaments in Italy, Spain, Switzerland, and Germany. I also participated in the *Bundesliga* interclub matches for 50-and-up seniors, playing as the "hired gun" for TC Wolfsberg (*TC* standing for "Tennis Club") in Pforzheim, about 15 minutes from Ettlingen. We played our inter-club matches using a format similar to matches between college teams—six singles and three doubles matches, each worth one point. An Italian team in Trento had signed me to play for their club as well.

The reason I was playing so much tennis—and hustling lessons—was that I needed the money. For the last decade or so, financial problems had trailed me like the rats and mice that followed the Pied Piper in nearby Hamelin. I was experiencing great difficulty supporting my wife, Margaret, and our two daughters from her previous marriage, as well as an assortment of alimony and child support payments, the fallout of two marriages that ended in divorce. Oh, and there was a boat deal that went sour back in Florida that I still hadn't resolved to the owner's satisfaction. But I always saw the glass as half full: the next deal, the next endorsement contract, the next summer camp, or the next teaching job would be the one to put my financial problems behind me once and for all.

I topped off the tub with some more hot water and recalled how Margaret and I had moved to Europe two years earlier when I accepted an offer to coach Simon Dawson, a promising British player. We flew to Nottingham, England, where I tutored Simon, a good kid who worked incredibly hard on the practice court with me. In matches, however, nerves bested him to the point where he could hardly hit a ball. I felt for the youngster and wished I could have played for him, but after a summer of spotty results in 2001, his parents made the decision to let me go.

Not to worry—I had several contacts in France. I worked the phones and got a teaching job at the Racing Club de France, one of the most prestigious sports clubs in and around Paris. Margaret found a charming apartment that was part of a bed-and-breakfast near Compiegne, where France surrendered to Hitler back in 1940. When I arrived in France, I experienced a huge hassle in getting a work permit. It seemed that the French authorities severely regulated who could teach tennis and who couldn't—probably a form of protectionism for their homegrown teaching pros. I rustled up a few lessons under the table, but I was making nowhere close to the money I needed to cover our expenses. I hid that information from Margaret because I did not want her to worry.

We needed transportation, so I shopped around and found a cheap Renault Clio for two thousand euros, or around $2,250. This ordinary two-door wasn't much to look at, but at least we could get around. Only one problem: I didn't have two thousand euros to hand over to the Renault owner. I explained my problem to him, promising that I would pay as soon as my lessons picked up. Maybe he remembered me from my years playing at Roland Garros (which would have been a miracle since I lasted to the second week of the French Open only one time), but for whatever reason, he relented and handed me the keys to his well-used car. A month or so later, when he asked where his money was, I stalled him with a fresh set of excuses. He got mad and called the gendarmes, who paid a visit to our apartment. Margaret, who speaks excellent French, listened to the police describe how I had failed to pay for our Renault, which was news to her.

Now it was Margaret's turn to get angry with me, since I had been hiding the truth from her. I backpedaled, as I always did in these predicaments, and came up with another brainstorm: I could borrow the money from the parents of one of the few boys I was teaching. I had no idea how I would pay this unsuspecting family the money I owed them, but at least I would get the Renault owner and the police off my back.

It soon became apparent that France was a closed shop and would never grant me the necessary work papers. But then Rodolf Hanchin, who owned a tennis academy near Basel, Switzerland, contacted me about coaching there. That sounded like a great idea on my end. We packed our belongings in our Renault and drove to Basel, where I began teaching juniors living at the academy. Margaret, who didn't have anything to do, would join me on the lesson court, helping me coach the students. I liked having an extra set of eyes, but the Swiss academy owner didn't appreciate my coaching with Margaret there. In the Swiss mentality, having my wife on the court was like having two people holding the steering wheel of a car: it was unnatural and didn't work. I felt differently, and when I came to Margaret's defense, Rodolf and I clashed. The academy owner retaliated by sabotaging my work permit to stay in Switzerland.

Time to work my contacts again. I called Jürgen Fassbender, a former No. 1–ranked German player from the seventies, and outlined my yearlong odyssey in Europe. "Jürgen, I need a job," I pleaded. "Can you help?"

Jürgen, whose command of English was excellent, turned thoughtful. "Roscoe, I'd love to help you," he said. "Come to Germany, and we will get you back on your feet."

"What about a work permit?" That had been a problem in France and Switzerland.

"Permits are not so difficult in Germany, and I can help you there. I still have connections, you know."

I was one grateful—and itinerant—tennis coach when Margaret and I pulled into Karlsruhe in southern Germany, where Jürgen owned a club with some hotel rooms. He gave us a room and then introduced me to several guys from nearby Pforzheim, a cute town in the Schwarzwald region—the Black Forest. These players formed the second-best 50-and-older interclub team in Germany— but they had designs on winning the *Bundesliga* senior division the next season. Would I like to play with them? Of course! Although they couldn't pay me much (*Bundesliga* first-league teams like TC Blau Weiss Neuss paid professional players ranked from 120 to 400 in the world a lot to play for them), I thought that playing for Pforzheim would help me establish my name in Germany, which could translate into more income-producing lessons.

After Jürgen got me registered with the German Tennis Federation, I began teaching a bit and entering big International Tennis Federation age-group tournaments. I won titles in Germany, Switzerland, Italy, and Spain in 2002, which made me the second-ranked fifties player in the world and No. 1 in Germany. My serve still had some zip to it, and senior players didn't like it when I took the net. They wanted me to stay back and chip the ball with them, but I had been charging the net since my junior days back in Lookout Mountain, Tennessee.

An Italian management company talked to me about giving clinics, and I received inquiries from club owners about exhibitions. Maybe winning senior tournaments would spring free an endorsement deal or two. Whatever was happening in Germany in the early summer of 2003, I felt like life was finally looking up after the setbacks in England, France, and Switzerland. I was teaching at two or three clubs in the Karlsruhe area, giving lessons for 30 euros, or around $35 an hour. That was all the market could bear because tennis participation had waned in Germany following the retirements of Boris Becker and Steffi Graf, but at least we were surviving.

Margaret felt settled enough to bring her two teenage twins, Lauren and Lindsey, over to Germany. They had been living with Margaret's parents in Humble, Texas, until our situation stabilized. We rented a cozy house in Ettlingen, not far from the clubs for which I was teaching, and enrolled the girls at Europaschule, an excellent international school.

I was about to pull the plug on my bath when I heard the doorbell ring. Margaret was still in bed, and the girls had already departed for school. Should I go to the trouble of drying myself and putting on some clothes to answer the front door? I had no idea who would be calling on us so early in the morning.

The doorbell sounded again—and kept ringing. The ringer's persistency unsettled me, and then a sense of dread filled my throat. *Polizei!* Three months earlier, two German detectives had dropped by Jürgen's club, and it wasn't a social call asking me how I was enjoying life in Germany. Instead, one of the detectives told me that they had an international warrant for my arrest stemming from my inability to pay a Florida man $35,000 for a boat I had purchased in 2000. They made me stay at Jürgen's club while the matter was being resolved. While I cooperated, I proclaimed my innocence during the entire three hours of questioning.

The first thing I did at Jürgen's club was call Rainer Schubert, an attorney and teammate on my *Bundesliga* team. When I explained my side of the situation, he called the prosecutor and said that I was "working" on a payment plan, noting that it was my complete desire to pay back all the owed monies. I just needed some time to get back on my feet, Rainer said on my behalf.

The promise-to-pay ploy worked once again, and I was released. But when I heard the front door ringing on this Wednesday morning, I had a sinking feeling that the same detectives were waiting for me. I toweled off and stepped hurriedly into a pair of Wrangler blue jeans and a red, white, and blue K-Swiss collared tennis shirt. As the doorbell kept sounding, I became very worried. It had to be *them*.

I ran to the third-floor window and peeked out. Standing at my front-door landing were the two detectives—the same ones who questioned me at Jürgen's club! *Think, think. What are your options?* We didn't have a back door, so that ruled out an escape, but where could I run anyway? I had about as much chance of escaping as I did of winning Wimbledon the following month.

An uneasy feeling settled in the pit of my stomach. I knew they were coming to take me away, and I feared I would never come back to this house again. With each step down the staircase, I had this foreboding sense that my past had finally caught up with me.

I slowly opened the wooden door, knowing who would be standing there. The pair of detectives, dressed in street clothes, stiffened to attention. "We have to take you at this time," said the one to my right, in English.

"I understand," I said, as I beckoned them to come inside. "Listen, can I finish getting dressed?"

"Of course," said one of the detectives.

I bounded up the stairs to the master bedroom, where Margaret was now fully awake and wondering who was at the front door.

"It's the police," I said. "They've come to get me."

"The boat?"

I nodded. We both knew this day was not a matter of *if* but *when*.

"Shall I call Rainer? Maybe he—"

"Good idea. Tell him they're taking me to the police station. Maybe he can talk to the prosecutor again."

Time was passing quickly. "Listen, I have to go," I said, drawing Margaret close. "I love you," I said, and then I kissed her. What a mess I had laid on her; she didn't deserve this. I had to find a way out of this jam, and it certainly wasn't my first. I had been in jams all my life, whether it was facing a break point on my serve or facing a creditor who wanted to be repaid money I owed him. More often than not, I wriggled off the hook.

I grabbed my wallet, cell phone, and passport and stuffed them into my pants pockets. I put on some socks and a pair of tennis shoes covered with red clay. "Bye, Honey," I said with as much cheerfulness as I could muster. "I'll let you know what happens."

The detectives were politely waiting for me at the landing. "Do you have your passport?" one inquired. I knew why he was asking; once I handed it over to the authorities, I could not flee the country.

"Right here," I replied, lifting the navy blue United States of America passport out of my back pocket.

"Then let's go."

Getting Nowhere Fast

The detectives had me sit in the rear of a silver BMW—all the cops have nice cars in Germany—for the leisurely drive to the police headquarters in Karlsruhe. "Do you mind if I make a few phone calls?" I asked, showing them my cell phone.

First, I called a couple of students to cancel my lessons that morning. *Ah, I don't think I can make it today . . .* Then I dialed Rainer Schubert, who said that Margaret had reached him with the news that I was being arrested by the authorities. "Listen, Roscoe, it doesn't look good," he said. "I just spoke with the prosecutor and got nowhere. He said that he was tired of your stories and tired of waiting for you to pay the money you owe on that boat."

"Rainer, I know that, but they're going to throw me in jail. They can't do that!"

"I'll do what I can from this end, but it's the prosecutor who makes the decision. He determines whether you will go to jail, not the judge. Hang in there."

The detectives escorted me to the receiving desk. I emptied my pockets: wallet, cell phone, cell phone charger, and passport. The items were put into an oversized envelope, which I signed for. They let me keep my gold wedding ring. I have to say that the German detectives were cordial to me.

I was led to an office to wait for what would happen next. After a half hour, a detective offered me a small sandwich—two thin slices of white bread with a slice of cheese. Since I hadn't eaten breakfast, I slowly ate my cheese sandwich. I wasn't offered anything to drink, however, nor did I ask for anything.

An earnest young German man came to see me. "Mr. Tanner, I have been assigned as your interpreter," he said in English.

"Pleased to meet you," I said. "What's going to happen?"

"We have an appointment to see the judge at 10:50 at the courthouse."

Leave it to the punctual Germans to schedule a hearing at precisely 10:50 A.M. "Where's the courthouse?" I asked.

"Not far from here. About a five-minute drive."

At 10:30, the policemen arrived for the drive to the courthouse. I wasn't led to a courtroom but rather the judge's chamber, which was a small office on the first floor. A large table dominated the room, and I was directed to sit at the table across from the judge with my interpreter at my right side. A clerk sat next to the judge, staring into a laptop, and a solemn-faced guard stood at the door.

The judge looked to be middle-aged and was dressed in a business suit—he wasn't wearing the traditional black robes. He shuffled a few papers and then began reading something in German—the charges against me, I figured. After a few sentences, the judge stopped and waited for the interpreter to translate. I was right: the judge was reading the charges, which were well known by me. He said that I was being arrested on the basis of an international warrant from the State of Florida for writing a bad check worth $35,000. The judge informed me that I would be extradited to the United States to face charges. "How do you plead, Mr. Tanner?"

"Not guilty, Your Honor," I said, not sure what the local protocol was in addressing judges. "I'm putting together a payment plan, and I plan to make full restitution for the boat I purchased in Florida. I just need some time, Your Honor. The only way I can pay back what I owe is to work, not go to jail."

My answer seemed to mollify the German judge, whose posture visibly relaxed. "I don't see why our American friends are so adamant about extraditing Mr. Tanner to Florida," he said. "I think we can get the matter straightened out to everyone's satisfaction."

For the first time in nearly three hours, I relaxed. Maybe I would stay out of jail after all. I had never been incarcerated before, but I had seen plenty of prison movies, like *Shawshank Redemption*, and I didn't want to find out firsthand what the experience would be like.

"What happens next?" I asked my interpreter.

"The judge says he will talk to the prosecutor, and then they will let you know what they decide. But he seems sympathetic to you. Until they decide, though, they are going to take you to a holding cell."

At 11:30 A.M., a pair of policemen directed me down a set of stairs to a basement where their keys opened a rusty solid steel door to reveal a . . . dungeon. *Just like in the movies.* No sooner had I stepped inside the windowless cell than the steel door clanged shut. The pungent smell of sweat and urine hit me like a furnace blast. In the dim light, I could see dingy walls covered with graffiti, and much of what was written appeared to be of the "F——Amerika" variety. Some were drawings related to Kosovo, and one person had drawn an American being hung by his neck with another American hunched over with a knife sticking out of his back. Stuff written in German appeared to be derogatory to Americans as well.

Looking around, I took stock of my surroundings as the gravity of what was happening crashed on my shoulders. No bed, no toilet, no reading material, no windows—nothing except a wooden chair and a light bulb. I glanced at my left wrist for the time, but my watch had become part of my "inventory."

So I sat.

Looked at my hands.

Stood up.

Read the graffiti.

Sat down again.

Crossed my legs.

Ran a hand through my hair.

Stood up and paced around the cell.

And thought about what I had done to land in an intolerable place like this.

2

Cell 155

June 18, 2003, Karlsruhe Courthouse, 2:42 P.M.

The Germans let me stew in that dank, smelly cell for around three hours. I don't know what I would have done if I had to go to the bathroom—probably relieve myself in a corner, I guess. When I heard keys opening the massive lock in that solid steel door, my spirits lifted.

Two policemen escorted me into the judge's office again, where the same cast was waiting for me. Immediately, I could tell that something had changed in the judge's disposition. Where he had been patient and understanding with me in the morning, now he looked like he couldn't wait to throw the book at me.

He began with a long discourse in German, which my interpreter deferred from translating for me. Then the judge cleared his throat and leaned over to me. "You," he said in English, "must go to prison." A thin smile of contentment came over his face.

Prison! What I had experienced in that grimy holding cell had been a warm-up for what was yet to come. "Can I make any phone calls?" I asked reflexively. I needed to call Margaret, and maybe Rainer had some news.

The judge, who had been in my face just moments before, relaxed after my interpreter made the request. "You can make phone calls when you get to the prison," he said. The judge asked for a sheet of letterhead, and my interpreter explained that the judge was writing the prison authorities to inform them that they should cooperate in letting me make phone calls.

The hearing was over. I expected to be handcuffed by the two policemen who came for me, but instead of reaching for their cuffs, they led me to a white van with a block-lettered POLIZEI stenciled in green on the side panel. Wire mesh separated the front seats from two rows of benches. I sat in the rear bench as we pulled out of the courtyard and onto the streets of Karlsruhe. Several pedestrians glanced at me, and I wondered what they were thinking about the prisoner—the reality was starting to hit me—sitting in the white police van.

The booking process at the Karlsruhe municipal jail took a few minutes. Two cops fingerprinted me, directed me to look straight into the camera for a mug shot, and performed another inventory of my possessions. They gave me back my watch—one that Margaret had purchased for me—but asked for my wedding ring, which seemed odd, but I wasn't in a position to argue. The prison authorities kept my cell phone, cell phone charger, passport, and wallet.

The policemen also verified how much money was in my wallet—a sum of 50 euros and change. "Would you like to put this money on your account?" one asked me.

I wasn't sure what that meant, but from the way he asked, it sounded like everyone said yes to such a request, so I nodded my head in the affirmative.

"This is for your food," one policeman said. From a small tub, he took out one medium-size bowl, a wooden cutting board, a pitcher, one spoon, one fork, and one not-too-sharp knife. Seeing the knife unsettled me. If I was given a knife, then every other prisoner in this joint had one as well. But I wasn't about to bring up that point to the jailers.

"When's dinner?" I asked. The only thing I had eaten was that thin cheese sandwich earlier that morning.

"You missed dinner. We try to get you some food. Otherwise, you eat tomorrow," was the cold reply.

"Can I make a phone call?"

"No, later maybe."

When I was finished with the intake processing, they led me to a nearby double cell, where three others were sitting behind bars. I was told that this would be a temporary stop for me until I was transferred to a double cell upstairs.

Leaving the air-conditioned intake offices for the holding cell was an interesting experience and a huge temperature change. The cellblock had to be 90 degrees—no air-conditioning here. Europe, in the summer of 2003, was in the midst of a sizzling heat wave that hadn't been seen since the days of Charlemagne. At least that's what the tabloids said. It took me a couple of moments to get my bearings; the air stank of sweat and body odor in the suffocating atmosphere.

I stepped inside my holding cell, clutching a burlap bag with my cutting board, pitcher, bowl, and utensils. The three men were watching a soccer game—*fussball* they call it in Germany—on a small color TV in the cell.

"Hi," I said sheepishly, interrupting the game.

"American?" said one in an accent that told me he was from the good old U.S. of A.

"Yes, just like you, right?"

"The name's Dray," he said, stretching out a hand.

"Roscoe," I replied.

Dray wanted to talk. We quickly got to the *Why are you in here?* questions. "They busted me for sneaking on the tram," he said, referring to the Karlsruhe streetcars.

"Surely they didn't throw you in here for not buying a tram ticket," I observed.

"No, this was like the 20th time. They sentenced me to 15 days in jail."

I heard a rumbling down the hall. A guard arrived with my dinner: six pieces of stale bread, tea in a large pitcher, and a bowl of dip. I accepted the food with a grateful smile, and then I spread some of the dip onto a piece of bread. It looked like a marinated herring dip that I once had back in the States. After one bite, however, I nearly gagged. *This is bad.* No more dinner for me.

My other two cellmates looked up. One was a German; the other guy was from Cameroon. None recognized me as Roscoe Tanner, the tennis player, and I wasn't about to volunteer that information.

The German guy, who looked like a successful businessman, spoke very good English. He told me that he had a home on Long Island, a vacation condo in Vail, and a house in Switzerland. *Switzerland's probably where you put all the money you embezzled,* I thought, although I had no way of knowing, of course. When he opined that he knew American law forward and backward, however, my ears perked up. I briefed him on the gist of my troubles, saying that the State of Florida had issued a warrant for my arrest for my writing a rubber check to purchase a boat.

"This one's easy," he said with a breezy air, as if we were discussing the differences among different brands of German beer. "You'll get extradited to the States, no problem, even though Germany and the United States don't see eye to eye on a lot of things today."

I knew what this German fellow was saying. At that time, there was this little thing called Operation Iraqi Freedom dominating the news, and the United States' decision to invade Iraq and overthrow Saddam Hussein was vastly unpopular in Germany—and the rest of Western Europe. "While Germany has said no to America on Iraq, in virtually every other category they are saying yes to the United States to try to negate that," the German said. "I hear that one of the things we have loosened up on is extraditing prisoners back to the States and cooperating in an extremely different way."

"Really?" I said. Obviously, this topic, which hadn't even been on my radar screen when I woke up this morning, now interested me. "How long will it take for me to be extradited?"

"Six months, maybe less if you have a lawyer. Do you have a lawyer?"

"Ah, no," I replied. Although Rainer was making some phone calls on my behalf as a friend, both of us knew that I didn't have the euros to officially hire him. "I can't afford one."

"Then you're going to be here for six months."

I gulped as the enormity of the fix I was in began weighing on my shoulders. *Six months!*

Our attention turned to the soccer game on TV. "Do all the jail cells come with TVs?" I asked. Everything I had ever heard about prison life boiled down to something about "three hots and a cot."

"You can rent one for 17 euros a month," the American said. "Our friend from Cameroon"—he nodded toward the African— "rented this one."

Interesting. We made small talk as the American and the German gave me a primer on jail life: we would be locked in our cells for 23 hours a day; the only time we could leave our cells was to visit the exercise yard—about the size of half a basketball court— for 1 hour a day; we got two showers a week; breakfast was at 7:00 A.M., lunch came at noon, and dinner was served at 5:30 P.M., but lunch was the main meal of the day. If you didn't want to rent a TV, you could listen to a radio provided free to each cell for the asking. Prisoners had access to a library, but all the books and magazines were in German.

I was digesting that information when a visitor arrived for me, a social worker who said I could make a phone call. A guard led me to an office where I dialed my daughter Lauren, who had a cell phone. She was still at school.

"Listen, Lauren, I'm being held at the jail here in Karlsruhe."

My statement was greeted with silence—and probably disbelief.

"I'll explain later, but tell Mom where I am. The social worker said because it's a holiday tomorrow, I have to wait until Friday before I can call again. Tell your mom I'll try Friday."

We exchanged pleasantries before I hung up. I felt so bad for Margaret because I had hidden so many things from her. Although I had been faithful to her, I hadn't been honest with her. She had put up with so much, and now this.

After my phone call, a new guard arrived with the news that my cell was ready. I gathered up my burlap bag, said good-bye to the three guys, and followed the guard through a maze of corridors before we passed through a set of steel doors where the main jail population was housed.

Instead of inmates leaning against steel bars with their hands poking out, each cell was closed off to the world via a steel door with a small flap for passing food through. The chipped and well-scratched doors needed a paint job.

I must have walked along the cell-lined corridor for one hundred feet when my guard stopped. My eyes glanced up at the number above the cell door—155. This would be my new home, and a feeling in my gut told me I would be here for a while. The guard reached for a key chain attached to his waist and swung open the door. A young Nigerian, who looked to be in his midtwenties, was perched on the top bunk, listening to German radio. He flashed an ivory smile toward me.

"Hello," I said sheepishly, not sure how much English this African knew. I stretched out my hand in greeting. "I'm Roscoe."

"Eddie," came the reply. "You American?"

"Yes, I am," I said, relieved that my cellmate and I had the King's English in common. Eddie seemed pretty friendly.

The door clanged shut, which prompted me to take a deep breath. *So this is it.* It really did feel like the first day of the rest of my life.

"Why are you here?" I asked Eddie, figuring that was a good icebreaker.

"I came here to play soccer, but I didn't have any papers to get into the country. I couldn't get any work, so I sold some drugs and got caught. But I'm not a drug dealer."

Not that I would have known any better, but Eddie didn't look like a drug dealer to me.

"How long have you been here?"

"Ten months."

I couldn't imagine being in this cell for 10 months. "How much longer will you be in here?"

Eddie patted his tummy, which had gone soft from nearly a year of inactivity. He didn't look to be in much shape to play competitive soccer. "I have no idea."

I looked around at my new surroundings. The cell looked about 10 feet long and 6 feet wide. A two-person bunk to my left took up most of the room. Thin mattresses were covered with white sheets, a brown woolen blanket, and a flat plastic pillow. Against the back wall were a toilet and a sink. To my right were a tiny desk and a chair. The dirty yellow walls were covered with colorful graffiti, just like in the dungeon. It seemed that those who scribbled on the walls had something against Americans being in Kosovo, Albania, Afghanistan, and Iraq.

"Why don't we get a TV?" I asked.

"I'd like to have a TV, but I don't have any money."

"I have 50 euros. How do we get one?"

"Push the button," he said, pointing to a button next to the cell door.

Five minutes later, a guard arrived at the door.

"Ja?"

Uh-oh. I was going to have to speak German. "I vant a TV," I said, hoping that would get my point across.

The guard chattered away in German, losing me quickly. I looked to Eddie for help. "He says it takes two days to get a TV unless you have an account."

"I think I left my money on account. Tell him that."

Eddie did as I requested, and the guard grunted and left. He returned an hour later with a small color TV—certainly smaller than a 13-inch model that you see in kitchens back in the States— but it was still a TV. The cell had a cable outlet, which was remarkable. We hooked it up, and I watched Eddie's eyes register a mixture of joy and wonder.

"Let's see what we get here," I said, as I waved the remote at the tiny screen. Man, there were a lot of channels to choose from. Channels 1 through 26 were German channels. Channels 4, 10, and 13 appeared to show movies in German. Sports channels were 17, 18, and 19.

Channels 27 and 28 were French TV, but then I hit the jackpot when I reached Channel 29. English! Music to my ears! Channel 29 was CNBC, beamed in from the United States via satellite. Channel 30 looked to be Germany's answer to the QVC shopping channel, but Channel 31 was another English channel, CNN International out of London. The news anchors spoke with a "prop-ah" British accent learned at Stratford-upon-Avon. The last channel, 32, was a German news channel.

Things were certainly looking up now. Since I had nothing to read and nothing else with which to occupy my time, I kept the TV on CNN and caught up with the news. When the international version of CNN showed hard news and features from American correspondents based in Atlanta, feelings of homesickness bubbled up within me. It made me want to get back to the United States to deal with my legal problems.

While I watched TV that night, a huge thought bounced around my head like a neon yellow tennis ball: *It's real now. You're in jail.* I had to face up to my money mismanagement and to the people I had ripped off over the years. This was something I had been tardy in doing. Then my thoughts turned in a different direction. Maybe I could handle this somehow without having to return to America. Maybe there was a way I could wiggle out of this fix I was in.

Watching news got boring after half an hour, so I flipped to a German movie. My German is *schlecht.* I can pick out words, and if I sit and watch a movie, I can usually figure out the gist of it. When I hung out at the tennis clubs, I sat with groups and listened to them speak German, and I could generally make out what they were saying. As for my adding something to the conversation, that was impossible because I couldn't form any meaningful sentences.

Around 11:00 P.M., the forgettable movie ended. Inmates could watch TV all night in their cells, if they wanted to, but I was cooked from the traumatic day, and Eddie was ready for sleep. He had staked out the top bunk before my arrival, so I had the lower bunk. We took turns relieving ourselves in the toilet before turning in, which didn't bother me since I had been in hundreds of locker rooms during my playing career. Once the lights went out, though, I heard all sorts of yelling throughout the jailhouse. Angry people screamed out in Russian—at least that's what it sounded like to my ears.

I was not looking forward to my first night in jail. At one time, maids would have turned up my bed and left a mint on my pillow. Not in this joint. My pillow was covered by plastic, and my rock-hard bed was maybe an inch thick. I had two sheets and a blanket, but I didn't need a blanket since it was like a Fourth of July heat wave in that cell. I lay on my back and felt the sweat bead on my forehead. Soon, I felt like I was lying in a pool of perspiration. My mind raced at 153 miles per hour, working overtime to match my new reality with my new surroundings. The first thing I needed to do was get ahold of Rainer in the morning. He would know which levers to push to spring me out of here.

I turned on my side, causing a noise as my face rubbed against the plastic pillowcase. I wondered whose germs had been left on the pillow. My sweaty head constantly slipped off the plastic material. I hadn't been this uncomfortable sleeping since Margaret and the girls and I slept in our car at Euro Disney outside of Paris, waiting for the park to open.

I tossed throughout the night and woke up feeling totally unrefreshed at 6:00 A.M. Eddie was still snoring. I reached over and turned on CNN, but I pressed the mute button right away. All the news seemed to be about Iraq and whether coalition forces would ever find Saddam or his sons, Uday and Qusay. *I've got to get out of here*, I thought. *I've got to get this done immediately.*

The guard arrived at 7:00 A.M. with the breakfast cart. His thick fingers handed me four small, hard rolls and a tin of butter through the flap; then he filled my pitcher with tea and left. I poured myself a glass of tea and took a sip. "Ugh, I can't handle this," I said to myself. The tea tasted like Sweet 'n' Low with some lukewarm tea mixed in. Way too sweet! I poured the rest of my pitcher into the toilet and filled it with water from the sink.

Breaking a couple of the rolls in half, I buttered them and took a few bites. Now, German bread is good, and one of the reasons it's good is that they don't put preservatives in it. But, for that same reason, it tends to get stale and hard after a few hours in the air. With each crunchy bite, that bread tasted more like Melba toast.

I was hungry, though, since I had only eaten a cheese sandwich at the police station and a bite or two of that awful dip the night before. I ate my hard-shell German *brot* in silence, further souring my mood.

At 8:00 A.M., the guard came by again and opened the door.

"What's happening?" I asked Eddie.

"Recreation. We can go outside for an hour."

I wasn't in the mood. "I don't want to go," I said.

"You don't? It's the only time we get to leave our cells all day."

"You go ahead."

I watched Eddie follow the guard out the door, which was immediately locked following his departure. In the silence, I lay down on my bed and sulked because I wanted out—not to some stupid rec hour, but out of that jail. Time passed by very . . . slowly. I had no books, nothing to read. When I flipped on the TV, nothing interested me on any of the 32 channels.

Eddie came back at 9:00, looking a little more chipper. He said he had talked with some of his African friends in the exercise yard. In the late morning, I turned on the TV again and channel surfed. Then I remembered: Margaret's favorite show was on, a soap opera on French TV called *Les Feux de l'Amour*, which translated means "The Fires of Love." The hour-long program was actually a dubbed version of the American soap opera *The Young and the Restless*.

I nearly cried as I watched the show, not because of the silly plot but because I knew Margaret was probably watching the same program. Another wave of melancholy washed over me, and I was still feeling very sorry for myself when the guard arrived with lunch. "*Essen*," he called out. Time to eat.

Eddie and I found our dishes and lined up behind the flap in the steel door. I sure hoped for something better than that awful dip.

I handed my plate through the slot, then I bent over and peeked through the opening. The guard ladled a large helping of stew on my plate and handed it back to me.

The brown stew looked pretty good. I could see chunks of beef, so that was a good sign.

"Hand him your bowl," Eddie directed.

I did as I was told and watched the guard flop a heaping spoonful of cooked noodles in my bowl.

"Where do you want your salad?" Eddie asked. He sure knew the ropes around here. I didn't want the salad mixed with my stew, so I motioned to the guard. He understood what to do. The guard gave me a helping of *grüner Salat* on top of my noodles, then added a dash of oil-and-vinegar dressing on top of the greens. When he held up his pitcher of tea, I shook my head no.

I sat on my bunk bed and regarded my first complete meal in two days. My salivary glands came alive, and at that moment, I could have eaten anything—as long as it wasn't that awful dip.

First, I forked the salad, since it rested on my noodles; the veggies tasted good. Then I turned over my plate of stew into the bowl of noodles, mixed everything up, and pretended I was dining on Hungarian goulash. It was a nice-sized portion, and the warm meal filled my stomach, so much so that I couldn't finish all my food.

"Eddie, what do you do with the leftovers?"

"I wouldn't throw them away. We don't get much good food for dinner, so I would save it for later."

I shrugged my shoulders. More local knowledge, I guess. I covered my bowl with the cutting board so the flies and bugs wouldn't get into it and put it under my bed.

My stomach suddenly gurgled, and I felt the growing pressure to . . . fart. My cheeks held in the air for a moment, but then the pressure became too great, so I let it go.

The stinky smell took over the small cell. "Sorry," I apologized, lifting a hand, "but I have to go to the bathroom now."

I looked at the white ceramic toilet next to my bunk, then up at Eddie, who was sitting on the edge of his bunk. "That's OK," he said. "Don't worry about it." He lay down on his bunk and turned his head toward the wall.

I had really done it now. This had to be the most humiliating event of my life—taking a dump in front of a stranger. I stood up and took some toilet paper and wiped the toilet seat. *Sorry, Eddie, no offense, but . . .* I unfastened my blue jeans, dropped my underwear, and seated myself on the throne. This was ridiculous, so much so that I became angry with myself. *Roscoe, this is your fault. You put yourself here. This isn't a joke anymore. This is the real deal. They aren't playing around.*

As I sat there in the midst of my bowel movement—with no privacy—my thoughts floated to my past. How could a son from a prominent Tennessee family, a graduate of Stanford University, and a world-famous tennis player end up in a German jail?

I had really blown it this time. Despite every advantage in life, despite every connection, despite winning millions of dollars of prize money, everything was gone.

My possessions.

My wife and daughters.

My house in Ettlingen.

My livelihood.

And now my dignity.

As I pondered what I had done to mess up my life so much, it all came back to me.

3

My First Serve

Roscoe Tanner, Lookout Mountain, Tennessee.

That's how I was identified on drawsheets, introduced before my matches, and recorded in six-point agate type in sports sections. In many ways, my identity has been tied to my hometown like an ankle weight: I'm known around the world as Roscoe Tanner from Lookout Mountain, Tennessee.

I'm proud of my roots, although it's been 35 years since I've actually lived in Lookout Mountain. Even today when I meet people, they often say, "Oh, you're from Lookout Mountain," which causes a smile to crease my lips because I'm confident they have *no* idea about where I grew up, but I don't mind. Some of my friends and family, however, *did* mind when Bud Collins, the *Boston Globe* reporter and the dean of tennis journalists, took some liberties with my Lookout Mountain upbringing early in my professional career. Writing through the lens of his Yankee eye, Bud painted a picture of this hillbilly tennis player named Roscoe Tanner, a straw-haired hayseed who bludgeoned the serve and ran around the court in bare feet with a corncob pipe pitched in his mouth.

I guess Bud's colorful description of me—which, I admit, was all in good fun—fit the establishmentarian stereotype of the day. Tennis players, dressed in their crisp whites, generally rose up from the ivy-covered country clubs of the Northeast or sun-splashed public parks of Southern California, hailing from hometowns such as Forest Hills, New York, or Pasadena, California, not from outposts like Lookout Mountain, Tennessee. I still run into people, though, who think I grew up in a backwoods holler where the locals ran around in cut-off pants that reached their ankles, sipping moonshine while shooting sawed-off shotguns into the air—in other words, people still fighting the Civil War.

Actually, Lookout Mountain was the site of an important Civil War battle. But first, I need to give you a geography lesson. Lookout Mountain, which overlooks Chattanooga, quickly rises nearly two thousand feet above the Tennessee Valley floor, its steep sides protruding to the sky. The mountain is surrounded on three sides by a near-vertical rock wall, which is the reason for a unique weather phenomenon. Usually in the fall, after a clear dawn, a layer of fog fills the valley below. That fog layer was there on November 23, 1863, when Union and Confederate forces clashed on the northern face of Lookout Mountain. The skirmish was given the poetic name of the "Battle Above the Clouds."

Today, there's a popular tourist attraction on top of Lookout Mountain called Rock City Gardens, which draws hundreds of thousands annually from miles around. Besides offering 10 acres of interesting rock formations and caverns, Rock City has a promontory—called Lover's Leap—where visitors can gaze out at seven states: Tennessee, Georgia, Alabama, Mississippi, South Carolina, North Carolina, and Virginia.

The predominant geographical feature viewed from Lover's Leap is the city of Chattanooga with the Tennessee River snaking through the city center. One hundred years ago Chattanooga was known as the "Dynamo of Dixie," an industrial city that served as the railway hub for the southeast. During the early 20th century, Chattanooga was poised to become *the* center of the South, but the city fathers didn't want the congestion of a major city, so they fought against expansion. An upstart called Atlanta, only 90 miles south, began aggressively courting business in the twenties and thirties, causing Chattanooga's star to lose some of its luster by the time I came on the scene in the fifties.

Fifty years ago, though, Chattanooga still had the highest number of manufacturing employees per capita of any city in the country—and major-league pollution. Because Chattanooga was situated in a bowl-like valley, the prevailing weather patterns trapped dirty air. Talk about muggy and hot in the summer! Steel foundries belched smoke into the sky, and auto-part factories dumped pollutants into the Tennessee River, which earned Chattanooga the dubious title of "Dirtiest City in America" in the sixties.

Lookout Mountain, perched 1,500 feet above Chattanooga, was 10 degrees cooler with more pristine air than that found in the valley below. The combination of striking views, cooler temperatures, and cleaner air helped Lookout Mountain become the well-to-do section of Chattanooga. Since the fifties, my hometown has evolved into a pricey suburb for the well-heeled professional class—successful businessmen, doctors, and lawyers.

My father, Leonard Roscoe Tanner Jr., was among the latter.

Family Ties

I was born on October 15, 1951, not a good tennis birthday. Up until a few years ago, junior players had to compete for the entire year in their age group. In other words, I was 13 years old for practically all of 1964 but had to play Boys 14-and-under events because I turned 14 later in the calendar year. If I were growing up today, I could play Boys 14 until I turned 15, which would give me nearly one more full year to compete against players the same age as me.

But I shouldn't complain. I'm fortunate to have been born at all. I was a caboose kid, a third child with two sisters considerably older than me; my sisters, Sherry and Wendy, were born 10 and 8 years before me, respectively. What happened is that my father,

Leonard, was the only son of an only son, so he knew the pressure was on to produce a male heir to carry on the family name. After two girls arrived, Dad was a bit gun-shy about trying again, but he and Mom gave it one last chance, and I came along.

My parents christened me Leonard Roscoe Tanner, the same name given to my father and grandfather. Both my dad and grandfather went by Leonard, although we grandkids called him "Pops." Grandfather used to call my father "Junior," but he didn't like that.

For some reason, I knew early on that I didn't want to be called "Leonard" or "Len." I was around four years old when I declared to Mom and Dad that I wanted to be known as Roscoe. I can't remember what they called me before that, although I remember my sisters saying "Roe Roe" to me. Maybe that's what I called myself as a toddler.

I never told Bud Collins this, but our first home was a little bitty log cabin on Lookout Mountain. Our family of five shared three bedrooms, and while our home was nothing fancy, my parents knew this would be a good neighborhood to raise a family. I don't remember seeing Dad that much growing up, though. He worked long hours to establish his fledgling law firm. I can remember Mom picking me up from school or tennis practice and swinging by the Volunteer Building, a 10-story "skyscraper" in downtown Chattanooga, where we would wait for him to take us out to dinner. We often waited . . . and waited . . . before he would come downstairs from his penthouse office.

Dad became a successful lawyer because he paid attention to details, and that attention to detail came out on the tennis court. He was a smart, meticulous player who lettered on the college tennis team at the University of Chattanooga. He had a real love for the game, which explains why he joined the two preeminent tennis clubs in town: the Manker-Patten Tennis Club, which became the Chattanooga Tennis Club in the seventies, and the Fairyland Club, located close to home on Lookout Mountain.

Dad got my sisters playing the game while I was still in diapers. Sherry was the first one to play tennis, but Wendy, the more competitive of the two sisters, became a little more proficient at the game. Dad liked to pit the two of them against each other to see who would come out on top, but all this maneuver did was turn Sherry against tennis. After losing one too many intramural matches to her younger sister, Sherry announced to the family that she was quitting tennis, and that's what she did.

Dad wised up when I became big enough to swing a tennis racket, which was made out of heavy wood in those days. The summer after first grade, he knew that I loved playing outdoors with three friends in the neighborhood: Forrest Simmons, Rob Healy, and King Oehmig. We were classroom buddies who played all the sports together. Football in the fall. Basketball in the winter. Sandlot baseball in the spring. Tennis and swimming in the summer.

I don't know whose idea it was for me to take tennis lessons, but my parents gladly agreed to having me join Forrest, Rob, and King for a weekly group lesson at the Fairyland Club. Now, I'm sure you're wondering how a tennis club got that name. Remember Rock City Gardens on top of Lookout Mountain? That tourist attraction and an adjoining subdivision, located on the Georgia side of Lookout Mountain, was started during the Great Depression years by Garnet and Frieda Carter, German immigrants who must have been inspired by Mother Goose. For instance, they named streets in their subdivision Little Red Riding Hood Lane, Cinderella Trail, and Peter Pan Road.

The pro at the Fairyland Club was a nice man named Jerry Evert, who had a brother in Florida, Jimmy, who was also a teaching pro. Jimmy had a tennis-playing family as well, including a daughter named Chris who became a very good player. At any rate, in the summer of 1958, Forrest, Rob, King, and I took our first series of group lessons together, and Mr. Evert made the game fun. I'll never forget how he taught us the basic motion for the serve. Instead of having us learn to serve on the tennis court, he led the four of us into the nearby woods.

I remember him positioning me underneath the leafy branch of an elm tree. "Roscoe, I want you to swing like this"—Mr. Evert mimicked a complete service motion—"and hit the leaf." Then he pointed to a low-lying leaf and instructed me to smack it. I would make a slow-motion service motion, speed up my swing, and knock the leaf off. Then I'd find another leaf to hit—I loved knocking defenseless leaves off trees. When we were back on the tennis court, my coach would say, "Toss the ball where the leaf was and hit it like a serve." And that is how I learned my service motion.

Since Mr. Evert made tennis so much fun, we couldn't get enough of the game during the summer months. In second and third grade, we were taking three or four group lessons a week from Mr. Evert. After we were finished, we would get a ride with him to the Manker-Patten Tennis Club, where he taught lessons in the afternoons. My friends and I would hang out at the club, either playing sets against each other, challenging each other to a Ping-Pong tournament, or walking to a nearby family market and buying double colas and moon pies—chocolate-covered cream patties.

Once Labor Day arrived, however, we put our wooden rackets back in their vises; the smell of fall leaves burning in the air meant that tennis season was over. The kids in the neighborhood moved on to backyard football and playground basketball. In the late spring, I played Little League baseball, but I was small for my age and a horrible hitter. My coach, Mr. Wann, instructed me to go up to home plate and crouch real low so that my strike zone was the size of a Mercedes hood ornament. I got walked all the time, but that didn't make baseball very enjoyable for me.

I liked the one-on-one aspect of tennis. Whether I won or lost was up to me, not someone else playing on my team. Dad signed me up to play my first sanctioned tournament when I was in fourth grade. I got creamed, 6–0, 6–0, but I won a few points, so I was pleased. That experience encouraged me to practice more and improve my game. I got better, but I was nothing compared to Zan Guerry, who was two years older than me. Zan had developed into one of the best 12-year-old juniors in the country. His tennis was guided by his father, Alex, a competitive player who was always looking to make tennis bigger and better in Chattanooga. Thus, it was big news when Mr. Guerry successfully lobbied the United States Lawn Tennis Association, as it was known back then, to move the National Boys 14 and Boys 12 events to the Manker-Patten Tennis Club.

The summer I was 10 years old, I received an invitation to play in the National Boys 12—not because I was any good, but because I was from Chattanooga and the tournament committee needed to fill out the draw. I drew the number-one seed in the first round, Alberto Carrero from Puerto Rico, so I was cannon fodder. They put me on a show court, and I was so hopped up that I played out of my mind the first game, which I won. Although I surrendered the next 12 games, winning a game against the tournament's top seed made it feel like a victory of sorts.

The next summer in the Boys 12 Nationals, Mr. Guerry arranged for me to practice the week before the tournament with a 10-year-old player from East St. Louis named Jimmy Connors. We were both not much taller than the height of the net, but my new practice partner was even smaller and skinnier than I was. All week long, Jimmy and I practiced every day at the Manker-Patten Tennis Club. His ground strokes were good, but he didn't have much power in his serve or overhead. He sure played with tremendous intensity on the court, like he had to win *every* point. I remember him playing a little better than me, but I was improving with each day.

While we practiced and played sets, Jimmy's mother and grand-mother paced about the court, correcting his technique, giving him pointers, and encouraging him to play steady. I would later learn that his mother, Gloria, was a teaching pro, so she knew the game, as did his grandmother, Bertha Thompson. Jimmy called his elders "One Mom" and "Two Mom."

I can tell you this: Jimmy Connors did whatever One Mom and Two Mom said. If Two Mom barked, "You're not going to the net anymore," he replied, "Yes, ma'am," and he camped himself on the baseline. If One Mom said, "Hit your spin serve," he kicked his serve into the box. If Two Mom announced that it was lunchtime and practice was over, he packed up his rackets. I never saw him question either one.

This was one *serious* tennis family. Me? Back in grammar school, tennis was just another sport to me, although my dad made it a dominant topic of our dinner table conversation. My parents, though, were also vitally interested in my schoolwork and my grades, and things like church and holidays were also important.

The same summer I was sparring against Jimmy Connors, we moved to a custom-built six-thousand-square-foot split-level home on East Brow Road. Mom, who wasn't educated as an architect, was an attentive and creative woman who felt confident enough to do the blueprints and act as the general contractor during construction of our two-story, brick-and-white-siding home. She was also quite a gardener, and she did a superb job of landscaping our two-acre plot of land. Although Mom had a gardener come by once a week to give her a hand, I was given the sweaty job of mowing our expansive lawns.

Mom was also really into decorating the house for the Thanksgiving and Christmas holidays. She loved cooking the traditional turkey-and-all-the-trimmings dinner for the family. Mom repeated the same Thanksgiving meal on Christmas Day, which was another big deal to her. I was a good eater who loved turkey drumsticks, mashed potatoes, corn on the cob, fruit salad, and my favorite dessert, vanilla ice cream with fresh strawberries.

You could say that holidays were huge for the Tanner clan. Every Christmas, Mom and Dad stuffed dozen of presents under the tree for my sisters and me. We opened our gifts for hours, and I squealed with delight when the wrapping paper gave way to a new toy—a Lionel train set, Lincoln Logs, or an erector set.

We had to finish opening our presents in time for the Christmas service at Lookout Mountain Presbyterian Church, a beautiful stone church about a block and a half away. Church was important to my parents, but more for the social aspects. I quickly learned the routine growing up: I had to dress in my "Sunday best"—navy blue blazer, white cotton shirt, striped tie, gray trousers, and shined shoes. Sunday school started at 9:00 A.M., followed by the church service at 11:00 A.M. Then it was on to brunch at the Fairyland Club, one of Chattanooga's oldest and most established private clubs with a stately Tudor clubhouse.

Brunch meant coats and ties for the men and spring dresses and hats for the women. It was a place to see and be seen. Although the buffet had everything a kid would want—prime rib, shrimp cocktail, fried chicken, and every salad under the sun—eating all that good food got old when your parents sat around and talked with their friends well into Sunday afternoon. We usually didn't leave the Fairyland Club until long after 2:00.

I went along with the program because it was expected of me. Every Sunday morning was the same: wake up, put on my nice clothes, go to Sunday school and church, and utilize my best manners at the Fairyland Club. The church part never meant that much to me. Oh, I learned some things about right and wrong, and how Jesus was born in a manger and died on a cross, but that was as far as it went for me—and for my parents. They didn't talk about God during the week, nor did I ever witness Mom or Dad praying and reading the Bible. We didn't go too deep, but neither did most of my friends at Lookout Mountain Presbyterian.

The only other church-related thing on our schedule was attending the Wednesday night potluck social in the church fellowship hall. Mom enjoyed making her deviled eggs, fried chicken, and fudge brownies and seeing her friends that evening.

In many respects, we were the All-American family through the early sixties. Mom was a stay-at-home mother, a June Cleaver type who wore pearls when she tended to her prized rose bushes and rock garden and loved raising her three children. Dad, too, was typical for the era: he was content to leave the bulk of the child raising to Mom while he worked long hours "for the family" as he climbed the ladder of success.

Since most of my interaction with him was related to my tennis, everything came to a head when I was 15 years old.

The Bet

In our family, I was taught that succeeding—winning—was paramount in life. As I entered my high school years, I had developed into one of the better players in Chattanooga. I had pretty-looking strokes, and club members told my parents that I hit the ball well, but we all knew that my hometown was a small pond in the junior tennis world. While I held my own in the South, when it came to stepping up at the national level, I was a crummy player.

During the summer after my freshman year of high school, I played four U.S. National events, traveling with Mom to far-flung locales such as Dallas, Texas; Burlingame, California; Louisville, Kentucky; and Kalamazoo, Michigan, to compete against the top players in my age-group. Each time, I lost in the first round of the main draw *and* in the first round of consolation. I was zero-for-eight for my first year in the Boys 16s, and after my last national tournament at Kalamazoo, I definitely had my tail between my legs.

Whenever I came home from an out-of-town tournament, Dad liked to invite me into the playroom to "discuss" how my matches went. He loved to analyze how things went with his lawyer's mind, but that got on my nerves as I grew older. I got sick of the way he dissected my matches, talked about strategy, about what I did well and what I did badly—especially when he hadn't seen the match for himself. I wouldn't say that he badgered the witness, but there wasn't a chance for rebuttal.

After my fourth national event without a win, Dad sat me down for another one of our painful discussions. From my point of view, there wasn't much to talk about. I had gotten hammered in Kalamazoo, and while I had tried my best, I wasn't good enough to win a match in the main draw or the consolation event. Dad didn't see things in the same light.

"Son, I noticed that you didn't do too well again," he said. "Just to let you know, your mother and I are pouring a lot of money into your tennis, but right now, there isn't much to show for it. Roscoe, I want you to realize that this is not a clambake."

I gathered up my courage to confront my father. "I'm sick and tired of sitting down with you after every tournament and having you evaluate me about what happened," I began. "I don't want to have any more discussions about my tennis. I just want to play my matches and do my thing. Give me a year to try that. I can win if you stop bugging me. In fact, I want to make a bet with you. If I win a national title next year, then you have to buy me a car."

Dad studied me for a moment. We both knew that I turned 16 the following October, meaning I was license eligible. His face warmed to the challenge. "Sure, Roscoe, I'll buy you a car—after you win a national title."

I'm sure my father resisted a smirk and an *Oh, yeah, like you're going to win a national crown after losing in the first round in singles and the consolation in all those tournaments this year.*

That winter, I played tennis year-round for the first time because the Manker-Patten Tennis Club had just constructed two indoor courts. What happened is that Mr. Guerry—looking out for Zan's tennis again—convinced the Manker-Patten Tennis Club that we needed indoor facilities if "our boys are going to compete with those Florida and California kids." Having only two courts at our disposal meant that I had to play at odd hours sometimes, 7:30 on Saturday mornings or after 9:00 on school nights, but I didn't mind. Most of the time I hit with Zan or guys on my high school tennis team.

I belonged to no ordinary tennis team. My parents sent me to Baylor School, at that time a private, boys-only military academy that offered a great—and expensive—college prep atmosphere. As for our tennis team, it seemed that Mr. Guerry wanted to assemble the top high school tennis team in the country at Baylor (which had dormitories for out-of-town students), so he single-handedly recruited enough good players for us to beat most Division 1 college teams.

His son, Zan, played number one, Antonio Ortiz from Puerto Rico was number two, I played number three, and Brian Gottfried, a hot player from Florida, was our number four guy. Mr. Guerry recruited other top players from the South: Joe Garcia from Knoxville, Tennessee; Bill Borders from Shreveport, Louisiana; and local boy David Dick. We were a powerhouse, winning every team match 9–0 without dropping a set.

In fact, during my junior and senior years of high school, Baylor School won the National Interscholastic Championships, an unofficial tournament drawing some of the best teams from around the country. Thanks to Mr. Guerry's influence, the National Interscholastics were held in—you guessed it—Chattanooga. At one point, our high school team won more than six hundred individual matches in a row.

With Dad honoring his promise to forgo critiquing my game, I felt like I made some big strides with my game. I also grew eight inches during my sophomore year of school; no longer was I handicapped with being a short, pudgy player. I became lean and tall enough to have the makings of a big serve. Still, I *know* I shocked the junior tennis scene when I captured the first U.S. National tournament held in 1967, the Boys 16 National Indoors at Market Hall in Dallas. Brian Gottfried and I swept the doubles crown as well.

Dad was stupefied, surprised, shell-shocked, and very happy to buy me a car—a 1965 white Pontiac Tempest with a red interior. I never heard a complaint out of his mouth. To show that my win wasn't a fluke, I won the Boys 16 National Hardcourts in Burlingame, a Northern California suburb, at the beginning of the summer. Woody Blocher and I also took the doubles title. Overnight, I was ranked fourth in the nation in the 16s, and my pair of national titles caught the attention of college coaches around the country.

This was an exciting development, of course, since it meant I could be awarded with a full-ride tennis scholarship at a good school. That was as far as we were thinking; in the late sixties nobody saw tennis as a career. Prior to 1968, the Grand Slam tournaments— the French Championships, Wimbledon, the U.S. Nationals, and the Australian Nationals—were not even open to professional players; only amateurs were allowed to participate. When professionals like Rod Laver and Ken Rosewall were finally allowed to step back on Wimbledon's Centre Court and Forest Hills stadium court, they weren't exactly bringing home the big bucks. Laver pocketed only £2,000 (around $3,500 in those days) for winning the first "open" Wimbledon in 1968.

Since there was little money in tennis, and because my father wanted me to become successful like him, he had my life all planned out. I would:

- attend a top school in the South, such as Duke or Vanderbilt
- earn my law degree at the University of Chicago Law School (where he had graduated from) or some other top law school
- pass the bar
- become a junior partner in his law firm, Tanner and Jahn
- marry the beautiful daughter of one of his friends at the Fairyland Club
- raise several kids (including at least one son to carry on the Tanner name)
- and live happily ever after in a nice home on Lookout Mountain.

That sounded fine to me since I had grown up enjoying the fruits of a comfortable upper-middle-class lifestyle.

Just before my senior year of high school, my parents moved into an even *nicer* residence on Lookout Mountain. Mom put on her contractor's hat again to oversee construction of their "dream home," a seven-thousand-square-foot white-column mansion located on one of the best lots on Lookout Mountain. Their new home on Gnome Trail was actually located on the Georgia side of Lookout Mountain. Just four hundred yards away from Rock City, our house sat on the brow of Lookout Mountain with a seven-state panorama. Dad prized that awesome view, and now he could behold that picturesque vista every day of the week and twice on Sunday. He and Mom built the home with an eye toward the future: they wanted plenty of room when the adult children and the grandkids visited. Sherry and Wendy, in their midtwenties, had found husbands. Sherry had married a young tennis-teaching professional named Ramsey Earnhart, which was ironic, given her lack of love for tennis. Wendy, after graduating from the University of Kentucky, had married Steve Miller, who was studying medicine at Johns Hopkins. I'm sure that Mom anticipated cooking those wonderful family dinners for Thanksgiving and Christmas.

Go West, Young Man

My parents and I knew that my choice of college would have an impact on my future in many ways, on and off the tennis court. I made things easier on Mom and Dad because I wasn't rebellious—except that time I told Dad to leave my tennis alone. I didn't grow my hair long or smoke dope or go off the deep end, which is rather remarkable for a teenager coming of age in the late sixties. I liked being a tennis player and blowing opponents off the court with my serve.

After winning those national titles, coaches flooded my mailbox with tons of letters, each one bidding me to join their program in

Florida, Texas, Arizona, or California. Of all the recruiting letters I received, the ones from Dick Gould, the head coach of the Stanford men's tennis team, stood out above the others. Mr. Gould's letters took a familiar tack: "Roscoe, you have the chance to start something by coming to Stanford. If you go to one of the other top colleges in tennis, you'll be another player in a long line of champions, but at Stanford . . ."

I was quite aware of the storied programs at the University of Southern California (where my brother-in-law Ramsey had been a three-time All-American) and UCLA in Los Angeles, Trinity and SMU in Texas, and the big state schools in the Southeastern Conference—Georgia, Alabama, and Florida. But Stanford was a mystery. All I knew was that coach Gould had just taken over a weak tennis program; Stanford hadn't had a good team since Ted Schroeder won the U.S. Intercollegiate *and* the U.S. Nationals (the U.S. Open today) in 1942. (Of course, this was back in the old amateur days, and World War II was going on.)

I visited more than a dozen schools in my junior and senior years of high school, including Stanford. I remember Dick Gould picking me up at San Francisco International and driving us into San Francisco. "Roscoe," he said as I picked through a crabmeat lunch on Fisherman's Wharf, "if you come to Stanford, you can think of yourself as the father of the program. You could be the start of something big."

I nodded, flattered that he thought so highly of me. When I returned home, I spoke glowingly of my visit to Stanford. Meanwhile, Dad had researched the Stanford Law School and learned of its sterling international reputation. "Roscoe, if you go to the University of Tennessee, you'd make contacts from this part of the world, but if you went to Stanford, you'd make contacts from all over the world. That could help you."

I agreed, but my parents and I also agreed it would be nice to have me close to home. The University of Tennessee was just down the road from Lookout Mountain, and while it couldn't compete academically with the Stanfords and Northwesterns of the world, the Volunteers weren't chopped liver either.

We decided to keep my options open as long as possible, figuring I could do that since I was the No. 1–ranked junior in the United States in 1969. Then three other top juniors and I discussed the idea of the four of us attending the University of Tennessee and creating an overnight powerhouse. They were my high school teammate, Brian Gottfried; my doubles partner, Woody Blocher; and a Pakistani living in the United States named Haroon Rahim.

As our idea took hold, I decided to join them at UT, so I signed a conference letter of intent. This meant I couldn't go anywhere in the Southeastern Conference except for Tennessee, but it did not bind me from changing my mind and accepting a scholarship from a school *outside* the SEC.

Still, I think all four of us were bound for Tennessee, until we found out that the coach, who made you live in an athletic dorm, woke you up every Saturday morning—year round, rain or shine—and made you run in front of his Volkswagen Bug until you threw up. Once I heard that story, I told my parents to forget Tennessee. My idea of a fun Saturday morning was sleeping in until it was time to go to the big football game. Brian, Woody, and Haroon went elsewhere, too.

So I began looking at Dick Gould's latest batch of recruiting letters with a new eye, and Stanford became more appealing with each passing day. The Farm, as it was called, felt familiar to me. I had traveled to the Bay Area for the national tournaments at Burlingame, plus I had stayed in the Stanford dorms the summer before my senior year when I was picked for the Junior Davis Cup team. The Junior Davis Cup program, sponsored by the United States Lawn Tennis Association, brought the country's best players to one place to train and spar against each other.

I knew Stanford was a great school, and the chance to be part of a new program appealed to me. Coach Gould was right: I could start something at Stanford.

With my parents' blessing, I said yes.

4

Down on the Farm

Coach Gould picked me up at the airport and drove me to my new home, Wilbur Hall on the Stanford campus.

I arrived to find the door to my dorm room swung wide open, where I got my first look at my new roommate cradling a black phone next to his left ear.

"Hang on a minute," he said into the phone. He extended his right arm. "Graeme McDonald," he said, shaking my hand. "Be right with you."

Graeme wore long, blond, curly hair and dark brown horn-rim glasses that were popular in the late sixties. A tobacco pipe hung from the side of his mouth, and he was wearing the Stanford uniform—white T-shirt and blue jeans. He turned his attention back to the phone; the fact that he had one already installed by the first day of college impressed me.

"I need four liters of Smirnoff, three bottles of Beefeater gin, and a dozen tonic waters," he said. "Do you have any limes? Excellent. Put everything on my parents' account. I'd like to have everything delivered to Stanford University. I'm on the first floor in the Arroyo section of Wilbur Hall. Room 107. Can you be here within the hour? Perfect."

It turned out that Graeme was from nearby Hillsborough, a well-to-do enclave dotted with mansions and long driveways. His

41

parents had an open account at a local liquor store, and Graeme was stocking up for our first weekend. Talk about perfection for a college freshman.

Our room turned out to be party central that first year. I wasn't a drinker—I was pretty serious about my tennis—but I often joined Graeme and the guys and gals for a sociable vodka and tonic before dinner. Fitting in was important to me, and it helped that I felt comfortable with my new surroundings and the college life.

I also felt comfortable going to church the first few Sunday mornings. A nondenominational service was held at 10:00 A.M. at the Leland Stanford Memorial Church, a Romanesque chapel with carved natural stone and striking stained-glass windows that reminded me of a mini–Notre Dame. Jane Stanford built this architectural crown jewel as a memorial to her late husband, Leland, back in 1903. The Stanfords, who had founded their private university 12 years earlier, were deeply religious people. Mrs. Stanford had this inscribed on one of the interior sandstone walls:

> Religion is intended as a comfort, a solace, a necessity to
> the soul's welfare; and whichever form of religion offers
> the greatest comfort, the greatest solace, it is the form
> which should be adopted, be its name what it will.

That about summed up my thoughts about religion. Going to church gave me comfort, a feeling that all was right with the world. Not that I had a deep faith or anything. I have to admit that I was attending the Stanford services because I had been trained all my life by my parents to go to church on Sunday mornings.

About a month after I arrived on the Stanford campus, I stayed out real late one Saturday night and slept in the following morning. I missed church for the first time, which prompted pangs of guilt. I eventually shrugged off those feelings, but when I slept in the following Sunday and skipped church a second time, I noticed that I didn't feel as guilty. It dawned on me that I had the freedom to go or not go to church. I could do whatever I wanted, and Mom and Dad weren't around to wake me up and say it was time to get dressed for church. I pretty much stopped attending the Stanford church services after that.

Looking back, I would say that the spiritual part of my life was important to me, but deep in my heart, I knew I was giving God a lot of lip service. All my life I had put him in a compartment and left him there. Everything else in my life took a back seat to my tennis. I was starting to realize that I was a good player who, with some hard work, could challenge the best players in the world.

There's Something Happening Here

In the midst of my first quarter on the Stanford campus, I remember walking out of my dorm with several Kramer Autograph wood rackets under my arms. I needed to get them strung up at the little shack underneath the Stanford tennis stadium. I turned a corner, when suddenly I saw a mass of antiwar protestors storming the ROTC building, pelting the windows with rocks and clashing with campus police. The pungent smell of tear gas hung in the air. I ducked into the bushes and watched the melee unfold.

The Stanford campus was shut down for three days as antiwar protestors and police clashed. A lady named Mrs. Cooley, who was a big supporter of the Stanford tennis program, called Dick Gould all worried that I and two other freshman recruits—Gery Groslimond and Rick Fisher—were spooked by the antiwar protests and would transfer to another school. She offered the three of us the run of her three-bedroom pool house, along with a fully stocked bar. "I don't want you boys breathing that tear gas," she said as she showed us to our rooms.

During the three-day shutdown of the Stanford campus, Gery, Rick, and I hung out, floated in the pool with an adult beverage in hand, and got some studying done. When we felt up to it, we hit some balls on her backyard court. I thought this was a great way to go to school.

Dick Gould needn't have worried about me leaving; I loved Stanford and the tennis program he was putting together. Throughout the sixties, either USC or UCLA won the NCAA title; they were the top dogs in the college ranks, but I felt they were about to get a little competition. One day during the winter quarter, I had finished playing a challenge match, so I sat in the grandstands with coach Gould while other challenge matches unfolded before us.

"How many times do we play USC and UCLA?" I asked. Those were the big matches for us. I wasn't interested in when we played Cal or Sacramento State.

"We play one of them twice and one of them three times," Coach answered.

That didn't make sense to me. "How's that?"

"Well, we play them home and home during the season, and then in the Pac-8 conference tournament, we'll play either USC or UCLA in the semifinals. After we lose, we'll play Washington for third place." Coach Gould spoke as if he was telling me something obvious—like the sun rose to the east of Hoover Tower.

"Do we have to lose?" I wondered. "Why can't we win and play the other team in the final?"

Years later, Dick Gould would tell me that was the first time he ever considered that we might someday beat UCLA or USC. He also told me years later that before I arrived, the Stanford varsity team was the *third* best team on campus: the intramural team and the graduate student team would have bested his men's team.

So I offered a challenge to Coach that afternoon: if we beat one of the big, bad L.A. schools, he had to take us out for a steak and champagne dinner. Coach said sure, but he didn't think it was possible. I think we surprised him during my freshman year when we lost 6–3 to UCLA and 5–4 to USC, which meant we were competitive.

I couldn't play in all the matches as a freshman, even though I was the No. 1 player on the team. The NCAA had just changed its rules that year allowing freshmen to play varsity athletics, but for some arcane reason, I wasn't eligible for every match. As coach Gould predicted, we lost to USC in the semifinals of the Pac-8 championships, which were being held at UCLA. And sure enough, the University of Washington was waiting to play us for third place.

Talk about anticlimactic. Nobody was up for playing Washington, so the night before our match, the team and I whooped it up in Westwood until well past midnight. The next morning, we began our six singles matches all at the same time. I was across the net from Dick Knight, a good college player, so when I fell behind in the first set, I wasn't too worried. Even if I lost, I figured someone else would pick me up. Well, everyone else must have been thinking the same thing because five out of Stanford's six players lost their first set. After Knight captured the opening set from me, coach Gould was so mad that he was spitting nails. He stormed onto my court, practically frothing at the mouth.

"Everyone's losing!" he bellowed, jabbing a finger into my chest as he backed me up against the fence. "Did you hear me? We're losing to Washington! You better get it done." And then he stormed off to read the riot act to the next guy.

We swept all six singles matches.

We were much more keen for the season-ending NCAA tournament, which in 1970 was held in Salt Lake City. Back in those days, the NCAA team championship was determined by how well players competed in a come-one, come-all singles and doubles tournament. In other words, your team received a point for every match a team member won in each event. You were allowed to enter four players into the 256-player singles draw and two teams in the 128-team doubles draw, so the longer you and your teammates stayed in the tournament, the more points you racked up.

I reached the semifinals of singles and doubles, and if I won both matches, Stanford would finish ahead of USC—and give coach Gould a huge recruiting advantage. The semis and finals were best-of-five sets in those days, and my singles opponent was Zdravko Mincek, who played for nearby BYU, Brigham Young University. Since we were playing in Salt Lake City, Mincek had a boisterous hometown crowd behind him.

Coach Gould left me with some direct advice before the match. "Don't do anything," he said. "Just play. Don't say a word. If you get ahead, you'll take the crowd out of the match." I wish it had been that easy. Mincek was a tough Yugoslav, and we battled into a fifth set before I prevailed, 10–8. The partisan crowd gave us a standing ovation because they had witnessed a great tennis match—and I had kept my mouth shut.

I had an hour to get ready for my doubles match against the fine USC team of Erik Van Dillen and George Taylor. My partner was Rob Rippner, a senior known for a bad knee and quick reflexes around the net. We both understood the stakes: if we won, Stanford would finish ahead of USC in the NCAA standings for the first time in nearly 30 years.

We battled Van Dillen and Taylor into the fifth set before eking out a service break to take a 5–4 lead with my serve coming up. Rip was so excited that he was practically hyperventilating during the changeover. "Roscoe, you're going to have to serve hard because I'm not going to touch anything," he vowed as he wiped his brow with a towel. "I'm too nervous to even hit the ball."

That's not what I wanted to hear. "Rip, I'm exhausted. This is my 10th set of the day. I'm supposed to serve, and you cross and take everything."

"I'm not touching anything."

On the first point, Van Dillen popped up a sitter return, shoulder high, one step to the right of Rippner. Rip did not even wiggle. We both watched the return float right by his head for a winner.

"Rip—" I said, motioning him to come over.

"I told you. I'm too nervous. I can't hit a ball."

"You can do it, Rob," I said, giving him a pat but realizing I wasn't going to get any help from my jittery partner. I walked back to the baseline knowing that I had to go all out on first *and* second serves, which I successfully did that day. When we won my serve and the match, coach Gould was so excited that he scaled the small fence behind our bench and bear-hugged us before we could give the USC players the traditional handshake.

The next day, I could hardly move. I lost in four sets to Jeff Borowiak of UCLA in the finals, and Rip and I were no match for Pat Cramer and Luis Garcia of the University of Miami. After 10 contested sets the day before, there was no gas left in the tank. I didn't feel too badly, though, because I was just a freshman. There was always next year.

Not Fixing to Die Rag

I had more than my tennis to worry about following my freshman year. There was a war going on, the Vietnam War, and Uncle Sam was drafting able-bodied young people my age. The Selective Service had begun a lottery to bring some fairness to what was a life-and-death decision for some of my peers.

When I turned 18, I was classified 1A by the Selective Service, meaning I was ripe for the picking by the U.S. Army—if I had a low lottery number. I discussed my options with my parents—I could have sought a school deferment, which would have delayed my eligibility for the draft by three or four years. We decided to take our chances. If I did receive a low lottery number and it looked like I would be drafted, my parents would contact some people in Chattanooga to see if I could get into the Army Reserve or Coast Guard. Not too many people my age really wanted to go to Vietnam.

My lottery came up on July 1, 1970. I was playing a tournament in Chattanooga that day against Pancho Walthall, a good player from Texas. Pancho was the same age as me, and we were well aware that both of our birth dates had been placed inside small capsules about the size of a pecan and deposited into a large, deep bowl with 363 other birth dates. A hand would reach into the bowl, and a birth date would be picked.

You didn't want your birthday to be picked early. The newspapers said that if you were in the top 100, you would be in Vietnam by the end of the year. Anyone from 100 to 150 was on the bubble.

Pancho and I were assigned to our court, but neither of us was thinking about tennis—birth dates were being picked in Washington, D.C., right at that moment. After the racket spin, I would hold serve easily, followed by Pancho holding serve easily. Neither one of us could concentrate. We reached 11–11 in the first set (this was the last year we didn't play tiebreaker sets) when a buddy of mine came running out to the court. He had been watching the lottery on the clubhouse TV with both our birth dates in hand.

"Roscoe, good news! You were 310."

I felt like I had won, well, the lottery.

"What about me?" Pancho asked.

"You were 150. Sorry."

A cloud came over Pancho's face. He was on the bubble.

We resumed our match, and it was like two different players had taken the court. I felt energized, like I had been given a new lease on life. Pancho played as meek as a lamb, dropping eight straight games to lose 13–11, 6–0.

When I returned to Stanford that fall for my sophomore season, something great happened. My teammate Gery Groslimond and I were strolling from the tennis courts over to the athletic department for a shower when we caught up with a young coed walking our direction.

Gery, the gregarious one, struck up a conversation with her, and I stayed quiet while he did all the talking. She sure was cute, though—petite with short, light brown hair, and from first blush, she appeared to have a sassy personality. She told us her name was Nancy Cook from nearby Fillmore and that she was a sophomore who had just transferred from Occidental College. She mentioned she was living in Florence Moore Hall.

I liked her smile, and my attraction buttons were definitely punched. She reminded me of my first girlfriend, Anne Clark, whom I had dated for two years during high school. Anne and I had tried to keep things going when I flew off to Stanford (and she remained in Tennessee), but the miles prevented us from seeing each other, so we drifted apart. Still, my heart hurt after we went our separate ways.

Now my heart was going boom-boom with Nancy . . . and she was available. I gathered up the courage to ask her out. When I spoke with Gery about my idea, we both realized that we hadn't given her our names while we walked together to the athletic department building. So we decided to play a little trick on her.

I called her on the phone and introduced myself.

"Hello, Nancy. This is Roscoe, the fellow who walked with you yesterday from the tennis courts. I was wondering if you would like to go out to dinner with me on Saturday night. It would be a double date with my friend Gery, whom you met yesterday, too."

"I don't think I'm doing anything, so that would be fine."

She said yes!

"Good. I'll come by your dorm and pick you up. Will 7:00 be OK?"

That sounded fine to her. When Saturday night arrived, both Gery and I approached her dorm room and knocked on the door. "We're here to pick you up," I said.

She looked at me, and then at Gery.

"And by the way, which one of us is Roscoe?" Gery asked.

Nancy shot a second glance toward us. "You are," she said, nodding toward my teammate.

We looked at each with knowing smirks. "That's right," Gery said.

"See, I knew all along," she said.

And the ruse was on.

The four of us hopped into Gery's car for the drive into San Francisco's North Beach, where we planned to eat at an Italian restaurant before tromping around Fisherman's Wharf.

I think Gery and I kept it up for another 30 minutes before we busted a gut. Nancy sure was embarrassed, but she was a good sport. That's how our relationship started, and we liked each other right away. It wasn't long before we were a couple.

During my winter and spring quarters, we took many of the same classes together since she was a political science major like me. I was missing a ton of classes because of my tennis, but she volunteered to take notes. I'm telling you, Nancy had a court reporter's gift for gathering fantastic word-for-word notes. Her note-taking abilities were so good that Rick Fisher signed up for the same classes as me when I said yes to sharing Nancy's notes.

Nancy and I had fun together, and we studied together, although I think we did more of the former and less of the latter. I could see myself marrying her some day. She would drop by to see me at the men's fraternity I had joined my sophomore year—Zeta Psi, which overlooked Lake Lagunita on the Stanford campus. We had a great house with great food, thanks to Edna the Wonder Cook. Zeta Psi was filled with the nonfootball jocks: baseball players, swimmers, golfers, and tennis players. We pulled our share of crazy stunts—like raiding the Sigma Alpha Epsilon fraternity house and pelting the walls with eggs and tomatoes—but we weren't the "Animal House" on campus. That distinction belonged to the Delta Tau Deltas, populated with burly football players.

Our tennis team was now composed of better players. Coach Gould had a great recruiting class coming in for my sophomore year, which included Alex "Sandy" Mayer, a talented player from Flushing, New York; Jim Delaney of Washington, D.C.; and Paul Sidone of Carmel, California. Meanwhile, UCLA figured to be tough again, since they had successfully wooed Jimmy Connors to the Westwood campus.

Sometime during the winter quarter, coach Gould called the team together before practice and introduced a fellow named Jim Stump. Coach said he was from an organization called Campus Crusade for Christ.

Jim made a low-key pitch inviting anyone to join him for a tennis team Bible study to be held once a week. Although the invitation didn't terribly excite me, I liked the idea of having at least *something* spiritual in my life now that I had stopped going to church on the Stanford campus. I began regularly attending the Stanford tennis team Bible studies and actually enjoyed them because Jim made stories and teachings from Scripture quite interesting. We would meet for about an hour before practice, sometimes in the tennis team shack underneath the old grandstands. On a few occasions, we huddled up at a quiet place on campus.

About half the team—five or six guys—participated during my sophomore year. Sandy Mayer, Rick Fisher, and Gery Groslimond were among the regulars. Compared to the dry Sunday morning services at the Leland Stanford Memorial Chapel, I found Jim's Bible studies to be a welcome tonic. I also liked the fellowship with the other players and the way it brought us closer together.

I have to hand it to coach Gould because he made Stanford tennis a happening thing my sophomore year. On a bright April weekend, we played USC and UCLA on consecutive days, and Coach pulled out all the stops. He recruited the zany Stanford Band and the cute cheerleaders with their red-and-white pom-poms to stir up some energy in the big grandstand behind courts 1, 2, and 3.

We *killed* the Southern California schools, whipping USC 8–1 and blanking the Bruins, 9–0. None of us had forgotten the steak-and-champagne bet with coach Gould. When reminded of our challenge, he said we could have the big party at his house. He'd provide everything, he said—except for the steak and champagne, which we thought was rather chintzy. I remember the hat being passed among the players to purchase the filet mignon and bottles of cheap Andre Champagne Brut. We had a great time, but we vowed to get back at coach Gould for not buying.

A couple of weeks later, the Stanford team was in Southern California to play an exhibition-type match at a nice club in Newport Beach. Afterward, coach Gould dropped the 12 of us off at the Jolly Roger while he joined some wealthy Stanford supporters at an expensive French restaurant.

This was our chance to even the score, since the Stanford tennis program would be reimbursing us for the meal. "What should we do, guys?" I asked.

"Why don't we order everything on the menu?" Rick Fisher said.

That's what he told the waiter. "Bring one of everything on the menu," Rick said, and we doubled over from laughter. It wasn't so funny a couple of hours later when our tummies were sore from eating so much, but we didn't mind.

Coach Gould nearly fainted when he saw the bill. When he sought an explanation, we replied that we were hungry. What could he do?

Coach shrugged it off because he knew we had become the dominant team in the tough Pac-8. Although we had blanked UCLA in our home match, the NCAA format (team versus team wouldn't happen until 1977) with players advancing in the singles and doubles draw negated any head-to-head advantage that we had over the Bruins. Sure enough, we faltered as a team and finished fifth while UCLA moved on to win the NCAA team competition.

I had a good tournament, but I lost in the NCAA finals to Jimmy Connors, and that bothered me. I had beaten Jimmy all five times I had played him in my last year in the Boys 18. Granted, he was a year younger than me, but going into the NCAAs, Jimmy wasn't even the No. 1 player at UCLA: Jeff Borowiak and Haroon Rahim played one-two for the Bruins. But Jimmy played a hot hand that week, and he decided to turn pro six months after pocketing the NCAA singles championship.

The Last Year

The NCAA championship and individual tournament my junior year was played at the University of Georgia, and I was seeded No. 1 going in. In the round of 16, my opponent was Danny Birchmore, a senior at the University of Georgia and a legend around the Athens campus.

The newspapers were all over the matchup. Sportswriters wrote that our "historic" match pitted two longtime rivals who didn't like each other, and sparks were sure to fly. I wondered what these writers were smoking. Danny and I may have had a rivalry back in the 12s and 14s, but we liked each other just fine. The newspaper hype spurred a large crowd to show up, though, and more than five thousand Georgia fans spread their blankets on the hillside behind our court.

Danny won the spin of the racket and elected to serve. He popped in a good first serve that I punched into the net—a forced error. The huge crowd rose in unison and cheered for five minutes while Danny and I looked at each other slack-jawed. During the din, I glanced through the fence toward coach Gould, who motioned me to come over.

"You're on your own, kid," he said. Then he turned on his heels to watch another round-of-16 match.

Gee, thanks a lot, Coach.

I ended up breaking Danny in that first game and winning in two sets, which kept the crowd quiet. In the semifinals, I played Dickie Stockton, representing Trinity University in San Antonio, Texas. The match was best of five on a sweltering afternoon, and after I won the third set to go up two sets to one, we were given a 10-minute break.

I retreated to the locker room, where a University of Georgia trainer took one look at my flushed face and announced, "We need to get your body temperature down." He then proceeded to put an ice pack on the back of my neck, which cooled me down all right, but when I walked on the court to resume play, I couldn't swivel my neck five degrees in either direction. It felt like I was wearing a neck brace.

There was no warm-up for the fourth set—just serve 'em up and go. I fell behind 4–0 in less than 10 minutes, which stopped my momentum cold. My neck finally loosened up in the fifth set, but I couldn't close Dickie out, losing 7–5 in the fifth. That bitter loss cost us the NCAA team title when Stockton went on to win the NCAA singles championship the following day, giving Trinity the NCAA title as well. Sandy Mayer and I won the NCAA doubles title, which gave Stanford second place in the team standings. I consoled myself with the knowledge that second in the country wasn't bad for a program that had been going in the wrong direction when coach Gould took the job in 1966.

Although I didn't win the NCAAs that year, I knew I was becoming a very good player. Following my freshman and sopho- more years, I had been part of the six-man U.S. Davis Cup reserve team, sponsored by the United States Lawn Tennis Association. We were the young players that the USLTA thought would someday be playing for the United States in Davis Cup competition. My status on the reserve Davis Cup team meant that I could get straight into the draws of the U.S. summer circuit—the tournaments featuring the Lavers, Rosewalls, and Newcombes of the world—even though I was still an amateur. Not having to play qualifying tournaments was nice.

In the summer of 1971, for instance, I played professional tour- naments in Columbus, Ohio; Cincinnati; Indianapolis; the Merion Club outside Philadelphia; the U.S. Open at Forest Hills; South Orange, New Jersey; and the Pacific Southwest in Los Angeles. I acquitted myself well, and I continued to play a handful of professional tournaments in the winter and spring of 1972, my junior year at Stanford. I was always home, though, when Stanford had a dual match against the top schools.

Playing all these professional tournaments earned me a world ranking in the top 25 that spring, and that's when I began to seriously think about turning pro. A fellow named Lamar Hunt, the owner of the Kansas City Chiefs football team, was a tennis nut, and he had started something called the WCT Tour. The purses were huge for the young professional game—$50,000 each week. The winners were collecting $10,000 checks, a princely sum in those days, but I was also aware that first-round losers received a check for $400, which barely covered expenses.

Although I was thinking about turning pro, I was still planning to become a lawyer. I viewed professional tennis as something exciting to do for a couple of years. I could see the world, compete on some of tennis' biggest stages, and when I was done, enroll in Stanford Law School. One thing I knew was that I couldn't juggle law school and the professional tour at the same time.

I sat down with coach Gould after the NCAAs in Athens. When I tossed out my idea of turning pro, he didn't try to talk me out of it even though I expressed reservations about leaving the team in a lurch. Coach put my mind at ease. "Roscoe, listen," he said. "We've had a great recruiting season. Pat DuPre and John Whitlinger signed letters of intent, and I don't know how we're going to play everybody. We're loaded."

He wasn't kidding. In 1973, the biggest competition for the Stanford men's team was the intrasquad matches to see who played on the top six. After winning its first NCAA title that year, the Stanford men's team became a juggernaut, collecting 15 titles over the next 30 years. The last time I saw coach Gould, he credited me with being the father of the resurgent Stanford program, but I reminded him that it was a team effort.

Coach Gould's words made me feel better about leaving Stanford, although I didn't plan to go very far. I wanted to earn my undergraduate degree on time; otherwise I could never become a lawyer. So at the end of my junior year, I came up with a game plan. Since I was a quarter ahead in academic credits, I would return to Stanford for the fall quarter, skip the winter quarter to play Lamar Hunt's WCT Tour, and return for the spring quarter and graduate with my class on time. Sure, I would have to pay for my Stanford tuition, but I was confident that professional tennis would be a better-than-break-even proposition.

My parents were thrilled with the idea. Dad thought it was a win-win situation: I could see how far I could go in tennis, pocket a few dollars, and then settle down at a law school of my choosing. Mom was plain proud.

Just two weeks after losing to Dickie Stockton in Athens, I notified the school and the pro tour that I wanted to become a touring professional. Wimbledon was fast approaching, and I needed to get on a plane for England.

On my way across the Atlantic, I was looking forward to what lay ahead—and not looking back.

5

Playing for Pay

Just as major league baseball players never forget their first hit, tennis players never forget their first professional match. Mine happened at the Queen's Club in London the week before the 1972 Wimbledon championships. After dropping the first set, I defeated a German player named Jürgen Fassbender—the same Jürgen Fassbender who would later help me find a teaching job in Germany—in the first round of Queen's Club. I won two more matches before losing to someone whose name I'll never forget: Pancho Gonzalez.

Ol' Pancho was old—44 to be exact—but he still had plenty of game to beat players half his age. Incredible, but I should have known that Pancho would play like a lion. The year before, Pancho had invited Jimmy Connors and me to work out with him in Las Vegas, where he was the head pro at Caesars Palace. This was my first trip to Las Vegas, and the garish neon and bright lights of the famous Strip dazzled this hillbilly kid from Lookout Mountain. The first day, we practiced hard under his experienced eye, and then he invited us for dinner at the Bacchanal Room, where we were served by harem girls who gave us shoulder massages at the end of the meal. Then it was off to the blackjack tables in the Caesars casino. There wasn't a clock anywhere in sight, so neither Jimmy nor I noticed the passage of time. After what seemed like a few hours of gambling, Pancho informed us that we would see him on the courts at 10:00 A.M. for a match against the Amritraj brothers, Vijay and Anand.

"Don't be late," he chuckled, and then we asked somebody what time it was.

"Eight o'clock," he said.

Jimmy and I looked at each other because we knew it wasn't 8:00 P.M. We had just two hours before we had to be on the court!

Pancho knew exactly what he was doing. He was teaching us that we had to watch what we did the night before a match. I learned something else from the Old Master that week: when you walk on the court, walk like you intend to win. Don't accept anything less.

Pancho taught me another lesson at Queen's Club—don't underestimate an older, more experienced player. "Got ya, kid," he said during the postmatch handshake, with a satisfied smile on his face. I shrugged my shoulders and realized I still had a ways to go as a pro, but at least now I was getting paid for my efforts. After my shower, I dropped by the tournament desk to collect my winnings. I looked down at my first check and gasped: £12.50. Then I did the math in my head. At the current exchange rate, I had just won 20 bucks.

A week later I played my first Wimbledon, and I acquitted myself well on the greensward, as they say in England. I lost in the third round to Colin Dibley and was handed another check—this time for £50. At this rate, I had enough money to pay for the cab fare to Heathrow Airport.

I came home for the U.S. summer circuit leading up to the U.S. Open, and the prize money was a little better. Sometime during August, I was home at Lookout Mountain between tournaments when the phone rang.

"Is this Roscoe Tanner?"

"Yes, it is."

"Hi. This is Arthur Ashe," the voice said.

Yeah, right. This had to be one of my old Zeta Psi buddies pulling a prank. I had never formally met Arthur Ashe. I think I had played him one time, but I certainly didn't know him. Why would one of the world's top five players go to the trouble to find out my home number and call little old me?

No one was going to pull one over on old Roscoe. "Hey, Artie baby," I jocularly said into the phone. "What's happenin'?"

I heard a throat clear. "Roscoe, I understand that you signed up to play on the WCT Tour next winter. I'm working on my schedule for next year, and I need a doubles partner. Would you like to play with me in 1973?"

Now I was convinced that someone was jerking my chain. No way the *real* Arthur Ashe would ask me to play doubles with him, so this had to be an imposter on the phone. But I decided to play along with the gag anyway. "Sure, Artie baby. Let's play together next year. You and I will make a good team," I said with a dollop of sarcasm.

The voice sounded a little confused. "All right," he said hesitantly. "I'll call Lamar Hunt and tell him we're going to play doubles together. They'll get in touch with you."

"Sure, Artie. You go right ahead and sign us up."

I'm sure I sounded like a jerk to Arthur, but he didn't say a word. After we said our good-byes, I hung up the phone, chuckling to myself.

The last laugh was on me. Two weeks later, a letter arrived in my mailbox from Lamar Hunt. He welcomed me to the WCT fold and then wrote the following sentence: "I just spoke with Arthur, and he said that you two would be playing doubles together. Allow me to be the first person to wish you and Arthur all the best as you compete against some of the top doubles teams in the world."

So it was true.

Later on, Arthur teased me pretty good over that auspicious introduction. Our first tournament together was in January 1973 at the Royal Albert Hall in London, a Victorian-era venue normally reserved for the London Philharmonic or opera singers like Beverly Sills. The tournament organizers had set up a temporary court—covered with carpet—over the floor seats and part of the massive stage. I certainly felt out of place when I warmed up and looked up to see tiers of private boxes in the gilded grand auditorium.

The Royal Albert Hall drew an upper-crust crowd: the male patrons were dressed in either formal black tie or dark business suits, and the women were adorned in elegant dresses and sequined gowns that you'd normally see at a charity ball. No wonder John Lennon, during the Beatles' first performance at the Royal Albert Hall, told the well-to-do audience that rather than clapping their hands, they could jangle their jewelry instead! Playing tennis inside this ritzy hall felt like a command performance for the queen at Buckingham Palace.

I walked into the locker room—actually, the backstage dressing room—to get ready for my first-round doubles match. The first people I saw were our opponents, the Australian team of Ken Rosewall and Fred Stolle, kibitzing in a corner. Both were players I had seen only on TV, so I averted my eyes; I held them in awe. Then I remembered Arthur telling me that I had to get over the hurdle of not putting the top players on a pedestal. "You have to learn to play the point, not the idol," he said.

John Newcombe, another guy I'd only seen on TV, dropped by with some breathtaking news. "Mates, you won't believe the bird in the mink coat sitting in the third row. She is absolutely stunning."

"That's Roscoe's date," Arthur piped up.

This was news to me. I didn't know that Arthur had arranged some female companionship for me after the match.

"She works at the Playboy Club as a bunny," Arthur explained, which set off a round of kidding from the Aussie contingent. I could see their imaginations working overtime, conjuring up images of cocktail waitresses with hourglass figures waltzing about in their Playboy bunny costumes: strapless form-fitting black outfits with satin bunny ears in their hair and fluffy tails on their backsides.

Arthur and I had gone out on the town the night before at the Playboy Club, where my doubles partner liked to gamble when he was in London. From the way people greeted him and treated him, Arthur seemed to be a regular there. He must have hustled a date for me when I wasn't looking.

"Great," I said, flashing a grin, but something inside felt funny. Arthur knew I was engaged to Nancy. I had asked her to marry me three months earlier at Stanford after I returned to school following my first summer as a pro. But Arthur felt at age 22 I was too young to get married, and he told me that I had a lot of life to live before I settled down.

When Arthur and I walked onto the court at the Royal Albert Hall for our first doubles match as a team, I shot a glance at the drop-dead gorgeous young woman wrapped in a mink coat. We made eye contact, and she smiled from her courtside seat. That relaxed me a bit, but it still took a while to settle into the match. After dropping the first set, Arthur and I rallied to build a 5–3 lead in the second set with my serve to come.

Now I knew how Rob Rippner felt. The idea that Arthur and I might actually *win* a set against one of the top doubles teams in the world caused me to suck wind as well. My legs felt like jelly, and my arms shivered with excitement. Arthur noticed the deer-in-the-headlights look.

He approached me with the cool detachment of a veteran who had been in this situation hundreds of times. "Roscoe, I've heard a lot about this famous serve of yours, but you haven't shown me anything yet. We're winning games, but you're not serving aces. I want four aces this game."

Are you joking? "Arthur, that's Rosewall and Stolle over there. You don't ace them. Let's just win the game and the set. How about that?"

"I want four aces," he repeated. Then he strolled up and took his place at the net.

The first point, I served an ace. The second point, another ace. On the third point, Stolle barely returned the ball over the net, which allowed Arthur to blast away a volley. My partner tsked-tsked and called me over. He put his arm around my shoulder and walked me back to the baseline. "I knew you couldn't do it," he deadpanned, and I cracked up. I liked being kidded by my new partner. Fully relaxed, I hit an unreturnable serve to claim the second set.

We played a tight third set but gained a service break at 5–4, my serve again. During the changeover, Arthur needled me. "You couldn't do it last time," he said, shaking his head. "I want to see four aces." He was serious.

"Arthur, I just want to win the match. This is Rosewall and Stolle we're talking about."

"Sorry. I want four aces."

I aced Stolle on the first point. I blew a first serve by Rosewall on the second point. I screamed another serve past a statue-like Stolle on the third point. Three aces had given us triple match point. Arthur turned around and nodded his approval. "One more," he said, and I knew what he was referring to. At 40–love, I cranked up another cannonball that Rosewall barely touched with the end of his racket. The ball skittered sideways into the second tier of box seats.

Arthur, with his hand extended, shook his head in mock disgust. "See, I knew you couldn't do it."

We shared a good laugh, and now my date was waiting for me. Any reservations that I had about going out with another woman while being engaged to Nancy flew out the window after meeting the shapely Playboy Bunny. I've long since forgotten her real name, but let's call her Elena. She said she was from Czechoslovakia, but all I could think about was how much Elena was a dead ringer for Hollywood sex kitten Raquel Welch.

I had a wonderful time with Elena as we went out for dinner and dancing in London's hopping West End. I justified my actions by reminding myself that since Elena and I didn't end up in bed that evening, it was OK to go out with her even though I had promised myself to Nancy.

Later on, my rationalizations would become harder to justify as I succumbed to the temptations of the tour. I was totally sucked in: having Arthur as my partner meant his friends were my friends, and his nightlife was my nightlife. All I had to do was follow Arthur to the required sponsor events, the top restaurants, and the hip nightclubs, and I witnessed beautiful women gravitating to him like he was James Bond. It didn't take much effort for me to pick up the leftovers.

I told myself I really shouldn't be doing this—ending up in hotel rooms with beautiful women I had met earlier that evening or earlier that week. At tour stops in Chicago, Washington, and Houston that winter, my "dates" weren't as chaste as my rendezvous with Elena in London. Just as I had found a way to compartmentalize my faith at Stanford, I had found a way to compartmentalize my behavior away from Nancy. No one could ever know that side of me, which became my little secret.

The Greatest Partner Ever

Back when I turned pro in 1972—and I know this is hard to believe—everyone played doubles. You had to; the few bucks you picked up in the doubles draw was sometimes the difference between making money that week and going further in the red. Your doubles partner was more than your on-court buddy: he was your practice partner, the guy who warmed you up before your singles match, and the friend who watched your back. Doubles partners traveled together, ate together, waited in locker rooms together, and sometimes slept together. By that, I mean they shared a hotel room to cut down on expenses.

Playing doubles and traveling with Arthur Ashe was one of the finest learning experiences anyone could ever have. We discussed everything—our opponents, tennis strategy, our love lives, politics, and anything else that might pop up. We became close companions who could tease each other like fraternity brothers.

A month after our debut at the Royal Albert Hall—we had beaten two more quality teams before losing in the finals to Tom Okker and Marty Riessen—we were playing in Cologne, then part of West Germany. The venue was a cold and sterile *hallenstadion*, where the locker-room floor was concrete and the room temperature was as cold as a meat locker. Arthur and I were changing out of street clothes for a doubles match when I looked down and saw that Arthur's feet were white from lack of circulation in the cool temperature.

"Arthur, look. You're a white guy. You're doing this black thing for money."

He started rubbing his feet. "No, I'm black, I'm black," he protested.

"No, you're not," I claimed with as straight a face as I could muster. Then we both burst out laughing.

One of Arthur's purest passions was trying to make life better for black people around the world. He was a reserved personality who hated to be out of control, but he very much wanted to help black people—in a manner he felt comfortable with. I can remember sitting in the locker room on numerous occasions when various black leaders would badger him to publicly speak out on civil rights matters. One time in Kingston, Jamaica, I witnessed one of the few occasions when Arthur lost his temper. A black leader from the Caribbean island was pressuring him to take a public stand on behalf of his cause—and step on a few white toes. "We need you out there, making our case. When are you coming out of your white world?" the Jamaican demanded in a loud voice. "Why can't you help us out?"

Arthur glared at him. "Because that's not who I am!" he said forcefully. From his travels and experience, Arthur understood that world leaders, corporate CEOs, and presidents reacted poorly to public pressure. They didn't like being backed into a corner and made to appear weak. Arthur intuitively understood this, which is why he quietly worked behind the scenes throughout much of his career.

I believe he did more to end apartheid in South Africa than he was ever given credit for. Although I never accompanied him to South Africa, I know a lot about what happened. He met with the highest government officials, including Prime Ministers B. J. Vorster and P. W. Botha, to move along programs that were more equitable to blacks and whites and doing something better for black South African kids.

Arthur always said that with the guys who were in power in South Africa, you could stand out in the streets of Johannesburg and protest all you want, but nothing would happen because they were stubborn as bricks. But if you go and meet with them—and don't tell anyone you're meeting with them—they can make moves, he believed.

Here in the United States, Arthur got to know the corporate leaders of dozens of major companies, and he used his back-channel influence to improve hiring programs and working conditions for black Americans. One of the companies that listened was Aetna Insurance, who were sponsors of the Aetna World Cup, a series of team matches between Australia and the United States in the seventies. That association led to private meetings with the Aetna board of directors, where he urged the leadership to develop a minority hiring program. Arthur never sought any credit for making that happen.

Some people criticized Arthur for being too calm on the court, and yes, he did have this aura of being under total control. But underneath that cool exterior, a furnace of desire burned. He wanted to win matches badly; he just didn't want to shake an umpire's stand to get a call reversed. If we'd get a bad call, he'd say to me, "Roscoe, we just got screwed. You go up and complain."

I wasn't so sure I should be the one arguing calls. "Arthur, you're one of the top players in the world, and I'm just a young guy coming out here. If I complain, they're not going to do anything. You're the one who carries weight."

"That's not the way I do things," he would say in a matter-of-fact tone. "I don't like to argue with the umpire, but I want you to defend us."

Arthur knew that I had fire in the belly as well. I had been nicknamed "Short Fuse" by South African player Ray Moore because when I was on the practice court, I could become very, very mad. I pushed myself hard in practice, and if things weren't happening the way I wanted them to, I exploded. Arthur knew all about that. "You complain for us. You're better at it."

"All right," I conceded. "But the least you can do is stand behind me when I go up to the umpire."

Arthur relented. "Sure, I can do that."

I looked at Arthur as the leader of our team, and I loved this special man. The fact that a black guy from Gum Springs, Virginia, and a white boy from Lookout Mountain, Tennessee, were playing together at the highest levels of the game was a remarkable turn of events for a game with a snobby country club history.

I also liked playing practical jokes on Arthur. The best one happened before the finals of a WCT event in Houston. The tournament was held at the River Oaks Country Club, one of those old-money private clubs populated with Texas blue bloods. Back then, River Oaks was sort of the last bastion of American whiteness. Please, this is not meant as a criticism (after all, I grew up in an all-white wealthy suburb of Chattanooga) but more as a way to describe the scene.

River Oaks was the last tournament of the WCT spring season, and a crazy idea came into my head for our doubles final. A really crazy idea.

"Arthur, I have to do something, but I'll be back in time for our match," I said.

Arthur shrugged his shoulders, and I scooted out of the locker room.

I asked a tournament volunteer to drive me to a nearby Kmart, where I purchased an Afro wig that was as big as a beach ball and stuff to paint my face black. Back in the car, I looked in the mirror and applied the blackface to my nose, cheeks, forehead, neck, and jowls, and then I donned the Afro wig.

The look was perfect.

When I walked into the locker room, Arthur's eyes got as big as basketballs. "You cannot be serious, Roscoe. You cannot be doing this."

"Yes, and now we match," I said, making fun of the WCT rule that doubles partners had to wear the same-colored shirts and matching shorts. "I'm ready to play. Let's go," I said with complete sincerity as I gathered up my racket bag.

Rod Laver, one of our opponents, got cramps from laughing so hard, but Arthur looked like a candidate for cardiac arrest. "I beg you, don't go on the court this way," he pleaded.

"It'll be OK," I soothed. "The crowd will love it."

Time for the prematch introductions, and Laver and his partner, Colin Dibley, were introduced first. They came running out to a full-stadium crowd that didn't understand why they were laughing their heads off. Then the public address announcer introduced Arthur, followed by me, which was the way I hoped things would go down.

I jogged onto the court in my Afro wig and blackface to cheers and clapping—which immediately stopped. You could hear a racket drop.

"Oh, no," Arthur whispered to Laver. "It's going to blow up now."

Then someone in the packed stadium tittered, and a few more guarded laughs could be heard. Suddenly the entire stadium was rollicking in laughter. Arthur didn't know what to do, but he was afraid to get near me. I got him perfect.

I kept the get-up on during the warm-up, but the Afro wig kept falling into my face, so I tossed it into my racket bag. I wiped most of the blackface off on a towel before the match, too.

Too bad we didn't win, but Laver and Dibley bested us that day, 4–6, 7–6, 6–4.

A Ring and a Date

After my winter stint with the WCT was over, I returned to Nancy's warm embrace and the Stanford campus for my final quarter. We had a whirlwind May coming up: Stanford graduation for the both of us and a wedding. We were young and in love and naïve, but that figures since we were both 22 years old.

Maybe Arthur was right—I was too young to get married—but I sensed that marrying Nancy was the right thing to do. I promised myself that I would stop sowing my wild oats after the nuptials. I respected the vows of marriage because I had seen that modeled in my parents back in Lookout Mountain.

We conducted the wedding ceremony before family and friends on May 28, 1973, at her parents' church in Fillmore, California. I had asked Jim Stump, the Stanford chaplain, to marry us. We honeymooned in the Bahamas, staying in Nassau and Eleuthera, taking our fill of love and walking along deserted beaches at sunset. I had the British grass court season coming up in less than two weeks and I wanted to stay in halfway decent shape, so I hit a few times with Leo Rolle, one of the top players on the island.

The Bahamas had been a British colony for 325 years, but the local newspapers were filled with stories about the Bahamas gaining independence from Great Britain on July 10, 1973. The sports pages contained another story that caught my eye: the top

I started playing tennis in grade school, and my mom had my tennis shirts monogrammed with "Roscoe." This photo was printed in a promotional brochure for the National 12s, which were played at my home club in Chattanooga, Tennessee. Joining me were Mary Navarre and Steve Parsons.

After failing to win a match at the national level, I made a bet with my father: if I won a national tournament, he would buy me a car. The following year, armed with my Jack Kramer wood rackets and a look of determination, I captured two titles in the National 16s and got my car, a 1965 white Pontiac Tempest.

Muttonchop sideburns, bead necklace—hey, it was the sixties! This shot was taken at the Chattanooga Tennis Club when I was 17 years old.

In 1969 I was the No. 1–ranked junior in the country. Here I'm practicing on my home courts at the Chattanooga Tennis Club.

I don't think anyone had seen Jimmy Connors so happy after losing to me at the Cal State Championships in 1969. I beat him five times that year, but he had my number in the pros.

I liked playing doubles, and my high school teammate, Brian Gottfried, and I won the National Hardcourt doubles crown at Burlingame, California, in 1969.

After winning the National Hardcourts, Brian Gottfried and I collected our hardware.

I'm flanked by my parents, Anne and Leonard, after being named Athlete of the Year by the Chattanooga Chamber of Commerce following my high school graduation.

While I was in high school, I was named to the U.S. Junior Davis Cup team, which gave me access to play and practice with the top juniors in the country. Miss Chattanooga was on hand to congratulate me.

The U.S. Junior Davis Cup team traveled to various tournaments during the summer, which provided me with loads of experience. I'm on the far left here, about to board a plane with (from left) Paul Gerken, Jeff Borowiak, captain Bob Potthast, and Mike Machette.

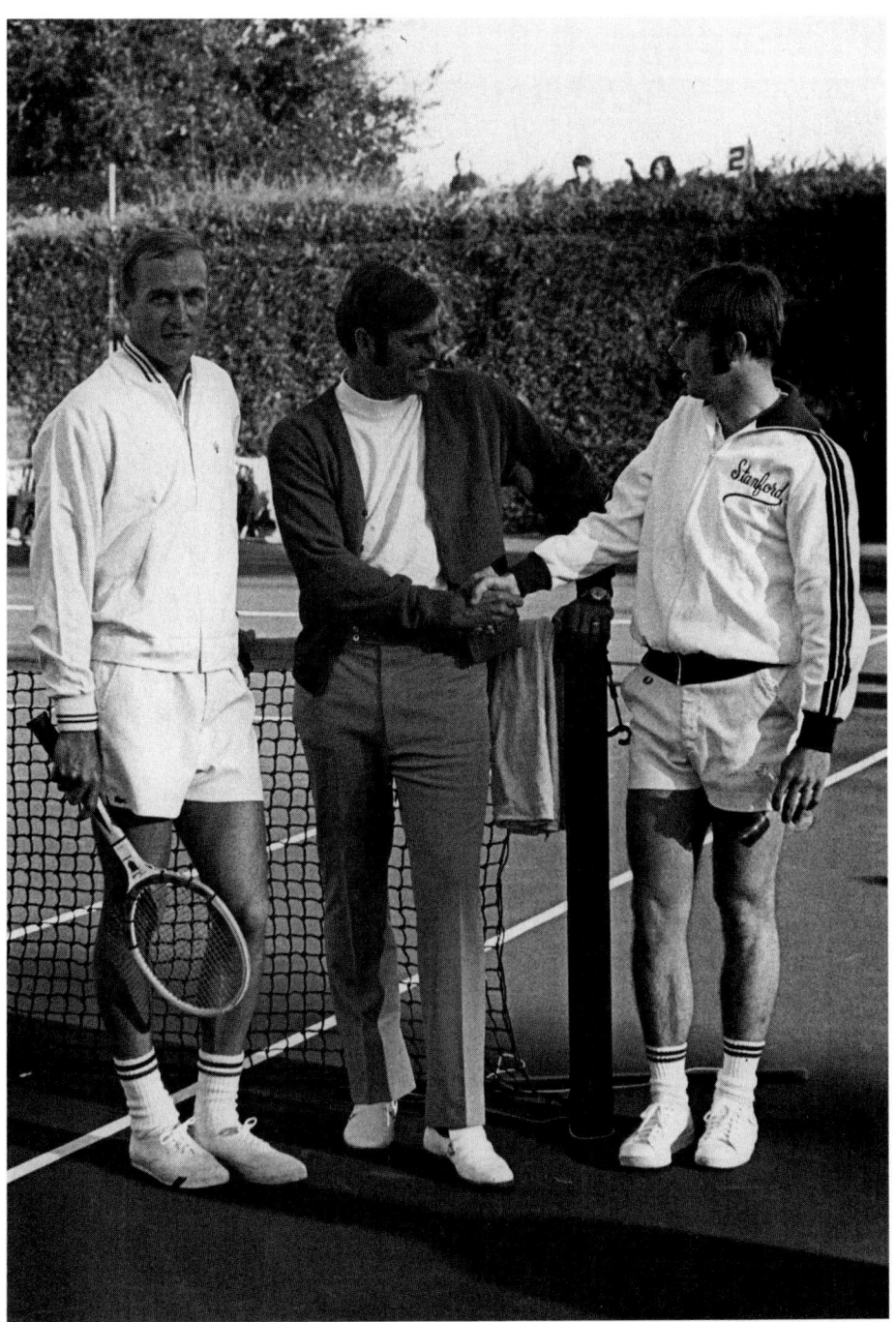

Dick Gould (center), coach of the Stanford tennis team, said that I could start something big by coming to Stanford, and he turned out to be prophetic. Coach Gould also thought outside the box and asked Stan Smith (left), one of the top players in the world, to play an exhibition match against me on the Stanford courts.

Wearing an Izod shirt with a Stanford logo, I won the U.S. Men's Amateur singles event with five tough sets over Haroon Rahim in the summer of 1970.

tennis players were talking about boycotting Wimbledon. "That's ridiculous," I told Nancy over breakfast one morning. "It'll never happen."

"Maybe we should check on it," she suggested, but I ignored her advice. I didn't see how we could skip Wimbledon. This was the biggest tournament on the calendar, a place where history was made.

From the Bahamas we flew to London and caught a train to Nottingham for a warm-up tournament. The first person I ran into was Tom Gorman, an American player.

"Why did you come to England?" he asked.

"What are you talking about? Wimbledon is in two weeks."

"We're not playing at Wimbledon."

"We're not?"

And then Tom explained the situation. The Yugoslav Tennis Federation was telling one of its players, Nikki Pilic, that if he didn't play Davis Cup for Yugoslavia, then he would be suspended from playing the Grand Slam events. The professional tennis community thought that was unfair because as a professional player, Pilic ought to have the choice of whether he plays Davis Cup. The impasse happened not long after the world's tennis pros formed a union called the Association of Tennis Professionals, or ATP. We decided to back Nikki Pilic, saying if he couldn't play Wimbledon, then we wouldn't play either.

A standoff occurred, but we did not back down. We boycotted Wimbledon that year, but the "championships" went on. The tournament committee filled the draw with non-ATP players: players from behind the Iron Curtain, Brits who weren't good enough to qualify for the Big W, and a handful of Americans who, for one reason or another, hadn't joined the ATP.

One of those players was my old doubles partner at Stanford: Sandy Mayer. He had a great run at Wimbledon, beating Jürgen Fassbender in the quarterfinals before losing to the Russian Alex

Metreveli in the semifinals. In what we called an all-Communist final, Jan Kodes of Czechoslovakia (whom I had beaten on the U.S. summer circuit the previous summer) took out Metreveli in straight sets.

It turned out that Nikki Pilic wasn't saying he didn't want to play Davis Cup for Yugoslavia; instead, he wanted more *money* to play for his country. We had backed him for the wrong reason, but it was the right thing to do. The successful boycott solidified the strength and power of the newly formed ATP.

The political infighting reflected the power struggle to control this new thing called "open tennis." Money was flowing into the game because tournaments were drawing big TV ratings and millions of new players were picking up the game. The media was calling it a "tennis boom," and sales of rackets, shoes, and clothes were increasing by 30 percent a year.

Why the boom? Think about what was happening demographically in the United States in 1973: the leading edge of the Baby Boomer generation was in their twenties, and they had discovered tennis. Technological advances in equipment had made the game easier to play: wooden rackets were giving way to aluminum and fiberglass models with larger, more forgiving heads and bigger sweet spots. White tennis balls, a symbol of tennis' country club past, were replaced with fluorescent yellow balls. Municipalities were building public tennis courts by the bushel, making the game affordable and available to the masses. All you needed to play tennis was a decent racket, a can of pressurized balls, and a partner. In addition, the monochromatic tennis whites had given way to vivid splashes of color, and Italian designers like Fila and Sergio Tacchini were infusing the game with fashionable clothes that looked good on and off the courts.

Tennis grew by leaps and bounds in the seventies. Men and women could easily play with each other, which was a social plus. People were attracted to a fiercely competitive game that was a marvelous physical activity filled with great mental stimulation. You didn't get bored playing tennis, and most saw improvement every time they stepped on the court. The sport of a lifetime, it was billed.

One more thing spurred the tennis boom years. Bobby Riggs, a 55-year-old senior player who had won Wimbledon back in 1939, lured Margaret Court, the top women's player, into playing him in 1973. He hustled her off the court, 6–2, 6–1, in the "Mother's Day Massacre." Suddenly, Bobby was crowing that he—someone with "one foot in the grave"—could beat any of the women's best players.

The whole thing was a farce, but suddenly *everyone* was talking about tennis. Chris Evert was asked to defend women's honor by giving Riggs a lesson, but she wanted no part of this circus. Billie Jean King, the first woman to make $100,000 playing sports, stepped up to the plate. In a match billed as the "libber versus the lobber," Billie Jean took on the male chauvinist pig, Bobby Riggs, before thirty thousand spectators in the Houston Astrodome and millions on TV. She won the "Battle of the Sexes" easily in three straight sets.

That was the wave that was building when I turned pro. As I began to challenge the best players in the world in 1973, I decided to paddle in and stand up as long as I could.

Law school would have to wait.

6

Taking to the Tour

The men's professional tennis tour in the early seventies wouldn't be recognizable to today's breed of players. The paucity of prize money supported one person on the road, not an entourage or even a coach. Some players traveled with a wife or girlfriend, but they could keep their expenses down by sharing a room at the players' hotel.

While we were all friendly with each other at the tournament site, the players tended to socialize away from the courts with those who shared their language. Americans and Australians and the occasional British player hung out together. The Spanish players were buddies with the South American and Mexican players. The French, Germans, and Italians kept to themselves even though we all stayed in the same hotel, where the tournament had arranged a discounted rate.

Socializing with the other players was a big part of the tour because we didn't have those big entourages. We would play our matches by day (and sometimes by night during the indoor season), go back to our hotel to shower, and meet at the hotel lobby before going out to dinner together. Then we'd come back to the hotel bar for a round of beers. The guys had a way of keeping track of whose turn it was to buy. "It's your shout," the Aussies would say when it was your turn to buy the next pitcher of beer. The routine was nearly the same every night, but those who were out of the tournament stayed up later than the marquee players who were advancing to the semis and finals.

A handful of British reporters followed the tour in those days— Richard Evans, Rex Bellamy, and Lance Tingay—and they were part of the evening social as well. But there was an unwritten rule that the press did not print anything they saw or heard at night unless they passed it by you first. Everything else was off the record.

They certainly would have had a lot to write about. We had colorful players by the dozen: rogues like Ilie Nastase and Ion Tiriac, legendary Aussies like Rod Laver, Ken Rosewall, Roy Emerson, and John Newcombe, heartthrobs like Bjorn Borg and Guillermo Vilas, homegrown players like Stan Smith and Bob Lutz, and arresting personalities like Jimmy Connors and Vitas Gerulaitis.

Ilie Nastase, who was always described in print as the "mercurial Romanian," was tennis' first bad boy in the Open era. His behavior was shocking, absolutely shocking, to the prim-and-proper tennis establishment. He was the first guy to moon the audience, spit at linesmen, and shake umpire chairs. He could curse in six different languages. He orchestrated chaos on the court and worked the crowd like a Vegas headliner. When you played against Ilie, you definitely felt like the supporting act. He controlled matches like a lion tamer with a chair and a whip.

"Nasty" was one of his printable nicknames, but my favorite one was thought up by Bud Collins, who called him the "Bucharest Buffoon" for his outrageous on-court antics. His partner in crime, fellow Romanian Ion Tiriac, once said that Ilie had a birdcage for a head with a cuckoo flying inside.

I think Ilie's cuckoo knew exactly what it was doing. When he pulled his stunts on the court, he understood that the ensuing controversy distracted his opponents and upset their concentration. Probably Ilie's biggest heist happened during the summer I turned pro, in 1972, at the U.S. Open final. I had a great tournament, coming out of nowhere to reach the quarterfinals, where I lost to Tom Gorman in five sets. If I had won, I would have played Nastase in the semifinals.

Ilie advanced to the finals, where my soon-to-be doubles partner, Arthur Ashe, awaited him, so I was vitally interested in the outcome. I was aghast by what transpired in the third-set tiebreaker, after the pair had split sets. When a call went against Nastase, he went crazy, throwing a towel at the linesman, and it wasn't a nice toss. Tiebreaker to Ashe.

After Ilie served out the first game of the fourth set, he turned and rifled a ball at the same linesman, showing that he was still ticked by the call in the tiebreaker. Predictably, the crowd gave him the Bronx cheer times 10.

The fans stayed on him until Arthur broke and held to go up 3–1 in the fourth. Ilie then gave the spectators a good look at his middle finger. More chaos ensued, and I could see Arthur trying to remain cool. Normally, when Arthur was up 4–3 serving on grass, the set was history, but not this time. Nasty had him rattled, and he sprinted past him to win in five sets and win his only U.S. Open championship.

"This is a great player," Arthur told the Forest Hills audience during the trophy presentation. "And when he brushes up on his court manners, he'll be even better."

Nastase's response? He gleefully waved his $25,000 winner's check at Arthur before slapping it on his forehead. A class act.

I remembered all this when I played Ilie for the first time two years later at the U.S. Open. My game was brimming with confidence; I had won my first pro tournament in Denver, and I thought I was ready to contend in the majors, three of which (Wimbledon, the U.S. Open, and the Australian Open) were still played on grass in those days. For the 1974 U.S. Open, I wasn't seeded in the top 16, but I thought I was a dangerous "floater" in the draw.

I drew Nastase in the round of 32, and Arthur reminded me that Ilie would pull all sorts of stuff. Sure enough, every time he had a break point on my serve, Ilie would hold up his hand while he talked to somebody in the grandstand. That somebody happened to be Alan King, a Las Vegas entertainer and big-time tennis fan.

This was getting more and more aggravating to Short Fuse. Not only was he driving me crazy with his stalling antics, but he *knew* he was getting under my skin. My concentration floated all over the place. I was down two sets to love and break point in the third when he stopped me again just as I was about to make my ball toss. Something inside me snapped.

"Ilie, come here," I said, as I walked to the net.

Nastase looked confused, and he gave me one of his famous "Who me?" looks. The crowd murmured because player-to-player confrontations didn't happen in a match.

"Come here," I motioned. Eventually, he took a few tentative steps and met me at the net.

"You listen to me," I began. "When I'm ready to serve, I don't want you holding up your hand so you can talk to your buddies. I know you're a big star, but if you do that one more time, I'm going to take my racket and smash your face."

"What are you talking about?"

"Just don't do it again. You got that?"

Nastase turned childlike, and he didn't say a thing. I'm sure he couldn't believe that this kid was standing up to him, Ilie Nastase. I'll tell you one thing: Ilie never held up his hand to stop me from serving again. This time, I rattled his cage because I came back from being down two sets to win in five sets.

My next big run-in with Ilie happened two years later during the 1976 spring season. The tour players had descended on Palm Springs, and Nasty was at his best—or worst. His entire repertoire was on display: throwing up his arms and causing uproars over line calls, dropping his pants, giving linesmen the finger, and shaking the umpire's stand—with a woman in the chair! His antics allowed him to snatch unlikely victories over Haroon Rahim and Dickie Stockton. I felt badly for my old college rivals, especially Dickie, who was on the receiving end of some nasty nicknames that played off his first name, if you catch my drift. Stockton had won the first set, but he was so upset that he lost the next two sets, 6–0, 7–6, in a bizarre finish.

The rules were not being enforced. Nastase would receive code violation after code violation from the umpire, and after the third warning, he was supposed to be defaulted. That didn't happen, probably because the umpires knew that the tournament director and the fans didn't want a gate attraction tossed out of the tournament.

After he stole the Stockton match, I was scheduled to play Nastase next in the quarterfinals. I happened to be riding in the transportation car with Ion Tiriac, Ilie's doubles partner and coach, and the topic of Ilie's controversial matches came up. In a rare moment of candor, Tiriac said, "He's going to do whatever he wants until somebody tells him to stop."

I knew exactly what he meant, since I had stood up to Ilie at the U.S. Open, but I was one of the few. Clark Graebner, an American player of note in the late sixties and early seventies, found himself across the net from Nastase at the Royal Albert Hall in 1972. When the usual fun and games started, Graebner hopped over the net and jabbed a pointed finger into Nastase's chest, warning him against trying any more dirty tricks. "I'm too frightened to continue," Nastase said, and defaulted.

This time I decided to take matters into my hands *before* the match. I found the tournament referee, Mr. Hardwick, and informed him that I would be carrying a rule book onto the court with me. "Look, I'm going to play this fair and square," I said, "but if Nastase gets his three warnings, on the next thing that he does, *I'm* quitting, so you will have to default one of us. I'm not going to be the dummy who stands out there and goes through all this and loses."

I was up 6–3, 3–1, taking care of business, when Nasty started his monkey business again. He'd already cursed the linesmen and shaken the umpire's chair, the usual stuff, for which he had received three warnings. At 15–40 on his serve, he generated some more commotion, and suddenly I saw Mr. Hardwick stepping onto the court. Nastase ran for cover in the stands, but Mr. Hardwick chased after him, trying to tell him something.

This is enough, I said to myself, and I walked over to my chair. I sat down and dramatically put my rackets away to show that I wasn't playing anymore. Then I pulled out my rule book from my racket bag and found the right page. I stood up to look for Mr. Hardwick, but he found me first. "No, no, Roscoe. I've done it this time. I've defaulted him."

I wasn't out to get Ilie. He could actually be funny sometimes, like the occasion when he hid Arthur's rackets just before they were to go out to play a big match. For Nastase, that was the height of hilarity. But one time Ilie got on the wrong side of a hefty Yugoslavian player named Zeljko Franulovic, a French Open finalist in 1970. Late in Zeljko's career, he suffered severe shoulder injuries in a car wreck. After doctors placed a pin in his shoulder, he started serving funny. We called him the Rusty Nail because he couldn't serve very well, but only Nastase would call him that to his face.

The story goes that at the French Open, Franulovic picked up Nastase and put him inside a locker and closed the door. Back then the lockers came with a wire mesh front so he could look out, and we could see him in there, begging us to let him out. Not even the attendants would come to his aid, and Ilie was stuck in that locker for a while.

After our encounter in Palm Springs, I think Ilie got the message. I played him several months later at the 1976 U.S. Open, but the surface had changed to clay at Forest Hills. We met up in the round of 16, but I was a big underdog because of the slow surface, which dulled the power of my serve. We split the first four sets of this night match played before a packed house, who were probably as surprised as I was that I was hanging tough against an experienced clay-court player.

New York crowds love an underdog, and they were cheering for me to beat Nastase, who was on his best behavior. At 4–4 in the fifth, Nastase had a break point on my serve. He crouched and readied himself for my delivery. After a short return, I approached the net and watched him line up a backhand down the line. He nailed it right at the line, but the linesman barked "Out!"

I wasn't sure if the ball was in or out, until I saw a distinct mark left on the Har-Tru court. The orb of the ball was half on the line and half out, and my heart sank. I knew it was good and that I couldn't take the point. I called for the linesman to check the mark, which prompted the crowd to go crazy. "Don't change the call!" I heard someone yell.

I had to. I informed the umpire that the ball was good.

"Game, Nastase," he said into the microphone. "He leads five games to four, final set."

I wish I could write that the tennis gods evened the score, that I broke Nastase back and came back to win. Didn't happen. Nastase held serve easily to win the match. But he shook my hand knowing that I had played fair, and that felt good to me.

It Was All About Me

I wish I had been as fair to those who loved me most—my wife, Nancy, and my family—as I was to Nastase. Professional tennis and the tour took over my life, probably because I thought I was pretty hot stuff. After all, I had beaten all the top players at one time or another, so it was only a matter of putting it all together at Wimbledon or the U.S. Open. Win either of those tournaments, and I would take my place among the legends of the game.

I pushed Nancy and my family aside because I was selfish. I didn't want to pay attention to their needs because I thought that would distract from my tennis. I felt that I was the most important person in their lives. I was the one winning those oversized checks that they hand to the winners—and they had gotten a lot bigger than £50. I was the one in the fishbowl, the player whom fans cheered, the media wanted to interview, and reporters wanted to write about. I justified my attitude and behavior by reminding myself that they didn't understand what I was going through.

Here's an example. One year at the Palm Springs tournament, my oldest sister, Sherry, and her husband, Ramsey, came out from Kansas City, Kansas, to see me play. They also wanted to visit with Stan Smith, who, like Ramsey, played at USC back in the sixties. Ramsey and Stan had become friends, even though Ramsey graduated three years before Stan arrived on the USC campus.

I threw a snit when I learned that Ramsey and Sherry were hanging out with Stan. He was one of my rivals, and I was brought up not to like my rivals. How inconsiderate of them! I decided that I would not have time for Ramsey and Sherry after that, a decision that created a chasm between us for many years.

Another time, Mom and Dad came up to the U.S. Open to watch me play. I'm sure they were proud as any parents would be in that situation, but did I go out of my way to see them? The answer is no. I disappeared after my matches to do my own thing. I was more important than them, I told myself, and so was my tennis. It grieves me to say that I did this to my parents, who sweated through my matches and undoubtedly lived and died with each point, but I blew them off after I reached the locker room.

And then there was Nancy. When we first got married, the travel was glamorous and the tour was exciting—for about the first year or two. She quickly figured out the score: the tennis world catered to me, not to her. For instance, when we arrived at a tournament site, she received a badge that said "Player Guest," not "Player Wife."

She heard condescending comments like, "Oh, you must be with Roscoe," or "Who are you?" Nor did she receive any support from other tour wives, who weren't necessarily friendly. Jealousy was rampant among the tour wives.

For the first three or four years of our marriage, Nancy subjugated her life for my tennis. The travel was tough since I was on the road 40 weeks a year. Those were full weeks because, by and large, I was playing into the weekends in either the singles or doubles draws, or both. Nancy spent a lot of time waiting around: waiting for her husband to practice, waiting for her husband to play his match, waiting for her husband to shower, and waiting with her husband for the next flight to board. Her self-worth was very much tied to how well I was performing on the tour, so she was the last one to receive any strokes from me or anyone else connected with professional tennis.

One incident probably summed up her experiences. It happened while I was playing a doubles match with Arthur in Boulder, Colorado, at an indoor arena. When Nancy watched my matches, she often became nervous and coped by unintentionally scooting around in her chair. On this occasion, she was sitting in a fold-up chair behind the court. As our match got progressively tighter, she steadily worked her chair to the back of a riser.

Suddenly, in the midst of a point, we heard a loud crash as black curtains from behind the court came crashing down. From behind the riser, Nancy's head popped up.

"Hey, Roscoe, your wife just fell on her butt!" Arthur cackled in a voice that everyone could hear. Nancy was so embarrassed, she slunk back down to the floor.

That's how Nancy felt she was treated by the tour life— dumped on. My wife tired of the grind after three or four years, and she began to stay home while I jetted off to some far-flung tournament. Little did she know, but that opened up the door for a whole lot of things to happen. You see, on the professional tennis circuit, you're very popular, and everyone knows where the tournament hotel is.

My Agent Man

One day during my first year with Arthur Ashe, he urged me to get an agent. He said that I had to look no further than Donald Dell. When I pressed him for more information, Arthur said that Donald had been a standout tennis player at Yale in the late fifties and had served as captain of the winning U.S. Davis Cup teams in 1968 and 1969, which Arthur had played on. Afterward, Arthur and Davis Cup teammate Stan Smith asked Donald, a well-regarded Washington, D.C., attorney, to represent them in their future professional careers. This led Dell to found ProServ, a sports marketing and management organization.

I met with Donald, immediately liked him, and asked him to represent me. The first thing he asked me was how much I was being paid to play with the Wilson Jack Kramer Autograph racket.

"Five hundred bucks a year," I said. That was the only company paying me to play with their products, so as far as I was concerned, getting that $500 was like finding money in the street.

Donald said he would review my deal with Wilson. A few weeks later, he told me that Wilson had agreed to rip up that contract and pay me $2,500 a year. Now I was rolling in the big dough!

I've already mentioned how Nancy and I traveled the circuit together early in our marriage. We literally lived out of suitcases because we didn't have a place of our own. When we did have an off week or two in the States, we stayed either at my parents' home in Lookout Mountain or with Nancy's parents in northern California. We talked about getting our own place, but Donald said that since we were on the road so much, it didn't make much sense to have a house.

That vaguely didn't sound right to me, and to Nancy, that was a non-starter. (At that time, I didn't understand a wife's need to have her own nest, a place she could call her own.) When we told Donald that we needed some sort of anchor in our lives, he suggested renting a condo that a partner of his owned on Amelia Island, the northernmost barrier island on Florida's Atlantic Coast. Establishing Florida residency was a smart financial move, he said, because there was no state income tax. That sounded like a swell idea to us, so we flew to Jacksonville, about a half hour from Amelia Island, and moved into our new place.

Poor Nancy. Our times in Amelia Island were glorified pit stops, and the dinky condo never felt like home. We needed our own retreat where we could tank up for the next big trip. A year later, we were in Los Angeles for a few days. Nancy and I had talked about relocating to Los Angeles because of its proximity to her family, a big international airport, and good players for me to train with.

I called a Stanford acquaintance, Jackie Douglas, who was selling real estate on L.A.'s West Side. "Jackie, Nancy and I have a few days here, and we'd like to look at a few houses in west L.A."

"What's your price range?" he asked.

"Oh, $250,000," I ventured, figuring that would be enough to get the ball rolling. This was the mid-seventies, and that was a lot of coin in those days.

I heard a long pause on the phone. "There's nothing available right now."

"You mean everything's sold."

"No, what I mean is that you can't buy anything in that price range, unless you're looking to buy a garage."

I thought a quarter of a million dollars was a lot of money. Back home, you could get a nice home on the brow of Lookout Mountain for that sum. I asked Jackie to take me around anyway and show me what things cost. It turned out that a half-decent home in Mandeville Canyon, for instance, would have been a cool $400,000.

That was too much money. Then I spoke with Dennis Ralston, a No. 1 player in the United States in the sixties and a fine pro player whose career was cut short by knee problems. I was making enough money to afford a coach, and I was thinking of asking Dennis to become mine. When I told him about our frustrating house-hunting experiences in west L.A., he said that real estate was much more affordable in the Palm Springs/Palm Desert area. Dennis was teaching tennis at the Sunrise Country Club in Rancho Mirage and would soon be moving to nearby Mission Hills.

Nancy and I hit Interstate 10 and combed through the home listings in the Palm Springs area. We found a nice single-family detached home not far from downtown. Better yet, it wasn't part of a development. The house came with a backyard pool and fully furnished for $75,000. That was a price more to our liking.

Some of my family members back in Tennessee asked how we could live in a desert where the summer temperatures regularly hit 115 degrees. I replied that we didn't figure to be home much at all during the summer months, and there was always air-conditioning. Nope, we told the family, the heat won't bother us.

Then Nancy tired of the travel and the role of "Player Guest." The world of professional tennis wasn't her world, and I didn't do enough to make her feel part of my world. As Nancy stayed home more and more, she was saying that she *preferred* the 115-degree heat to the hot glare of the pro tour.

She gave me an opening, and like the professional tennis player I was trained to be, I pounced on it. I just had to make sure that she never found out about the other women.

7

Breakfast at Wimbledon

By today's standards, I enjoyed a long, successful career between the white lines of a tennis court. After competing on the professional tennis circuit for 12 years, I retired in 1984 at the age of 32 when my left elbow could no longer handle the demands I placed on it. I always felt that I was more than a one-dimensional player, but once my serve lost its pop, I lost to players whom I used to crunch in straight sets. It was time to go do something else.

The record book shows that I played 866 matches and won two-thirds of them to post a 583–283 win-loss record. As I look over the arc of my career, a handful of those matches stand out. I would like to go into greater detail here, since they set the stage for what happened *after* I walked away from the game.

1975 Wimbledon

Mom and Dad joined Nancy and me for the trip to jolly old England, and one day when Mom came back to our hotel, a message from Buckingham Palace was waiting for her. It seemed that the secretary to the Queen Mother, after watching me advance through the Wimbledon draw on the telly, wondered if we were related to Lord Tanner, a member of British royalty.

Mom knew our family history well. She was aware that the Tanner ancestry dated back to the early settlers of Virginia who came across the Atlantic Ocean from England in the 17th century. After some discussion, the secretary and Mom agreed that a branch of our family *was* related to Lord Tanner. When Mom told me the good news, I expected some sort of door prize—or at least an invitation for tea and scones with the Queen Mother—but that never materialized.

Everyone was talking about Jimmy Connors in 1975, and rightly so. He was the defending champion, coming off probably the greatest year in the Open era. He won 99 matches and lost only 4 in 1974, winning 15 tournaments, including 3 Grand Slams: Australia, Wimbledon, and the U.S. Open. He wasn't allowed to enter the French Open because the French Tennis Federation banned Jimmy for playing World Team Tennis during the European spring clay-court season. We'll never know if Jimmy could have won the Grand Slam in 1974.

Jimmy separated himself from the other tennis pros in more ways than just the rankings. He didn't stay in the same hotel as the other players, which meant he didn't socialize with us either. He was one of the first to have an entourage, consisting of a coach (Pancho Segura), his mother (Gloria, or One Mom), a girlfriend (when he and Chris Evert were engaged in 1974), a good friend (Lornie Kuhle), and a few hangers-on. Jimmy's only friend on the tour was Ilie Nastase, if that tells you anything.

Jimmy definitely went out of his way to go his own way: he refused to boycott Wimbledon with us in 1973 or join the Association of Tennis Professionals (ATP). To add insult to injury, he had filed a multimillion-dollar lawsuit against the players' union. None of this seemed to hurt his tennis game, though. He had an unbelievable way of raising his level of play when it counted most. Jimmy was No. 1 by a landslide going into Wimbledon, and at the age of 22, he and his steel wand—the Wilson T2000—looked to rule the game for a long time.

I began my 1975 Wimbledon by beating Bob Lutz, Victor Pecci, Charlie Owens, and Mike Estep. I was seeded eleventh, and in my quarter of the draw was Guillermo Vilas, the lefty Argentine seeded fourth. For someone who grew up on slow dirt courts, Guillermo was a tough grass-courter; I didn't subdue him until the fifth set, which I won 6–2.

We played on Centre Court, and the English tabloids had fun taking pictures of a funny incident during the match. It seems that I smacked a serve with so much heat that it broke the head off Guillermo's racket; his frame literally snapped in two at the throat. The crowd enjoyed a hearty laugh at Guillermo's expense, who was a good sport about it. Even the Argentine had to smile as he retrieved the head of his racket from the grass.

It wasn't any laughing matter, though, when I found out who was waiting for me in the semifinals—ol' Jimbo himself. In the other half of the draw, my doubles partner Arthur Ashe would play Tony Roche, a sneaky, fast Australian left-hander with a classic serve-and-volley game and probably the best backhand volley in tennis.

I didn't fear Connors at all. Respected him, yes. Appreciated his focused determination. But I had known Jimmy since elementary school when we trained together at the Manker-Patten Tennis Club. All through the juniors, I had beaten him, so it wasn't like I was shaking in my sneakers. Still, I knew he had taken his game to a stratospheric level because he was beating the brains out of everyone he played. To subdue the world's No. 1, I would have to mix my serves around the box but also serve into the body so that Jimmy would have to block his returns back—and not have room to reach out and attack my serve. When I approached the net, I had to keep the ball up the middle so that he wouldn't have an angle to pass me.

The night before our semifinal matches, Arthur and I discussed strategy over a pasta dinner in London. "Here's how you play Jimmy," he said, and my ears perked up. I figured two minds were better than one. "You have to get him to hit soft balls, so don't be afraid to take pace off your shots," Arthur said. "When you approach the net, hit short and angular so that you can get him wide off the court."

"In other words, dink him around a bit," I offered, trying to understand what this looked like.

"Right," Arthur said. "He feeds off pace, so don't give him any. Jimmy doesn't like to generate speed. He doesn't do as well when he has to take extra steps to the ball, especially with that two-handed backhand of his. He doesn't have the reach with a two-handed grip."

I listened as if this oracle had dropped into my lap from Mount Olympus. The next day, I followed Arthur's advice to the letter. I angled off first volleys, instead of directing them deep toward the middle of the court. The trouble is my angle volley lacked depth and . . . angle. Jimmy ran them down and passed me easily on numerous occasions. When I fed him soft balls from the backcourt, he pounced on them and charged the net. Nothing in Arthur's game plan worked that afternoon on Centre Court. In about 45 minutes, he had won the first two sets, 6–4, 6–1.

I had a changeover following the second set. I decided that it was time to go back to my bullheaded game, serving big and punching my volleys with authority, which, I should have realized, was what got me into the Wimbledon semifinals in the first place. Throughout the third set, I played Connors tough, but he eked out the first break, and that was enough to close me out, 6–4, 6–1, 6–4.

"What happened?" Arthur asked in the locker room.

"Connors blew me off the court. Arthur, that's not my game, angling off volleys. He ate me up. By the time I got going, I was already down two sets."

Arthur looked pensive. He had just beaten Roche in five tough sets, and in two days, he would play in his first Wimbledon final. Arthur was 31, so he knew this would be his only chance. He also knew that *nobody* thought he was capable of defeating Jimmy Connors, who hadn't dropped a set in his six matches leading up to the final. Frankly, he looked unbeatable. London bookmakers declared Connors a prohibitive 10–1 favorite.

Arthur met with our agent, Donald Dell, and several players— Charlie Pasarell, Marty Riessen, and Fred McNair—to discuss strategy the night before. Obviously, they had witnessed the carnage, and everyone knew that Arthur played a power game similar to mine, albeit with some important differences. Arthur was still insisting that Connors could be beaten by feeding him junk and angling him off the court. Then the brain trust came up with an important wrinkle to the game plan: have Arthur hook his right-handed serve wide to Jimbo's two-handed backhand in the deuce court. That would open up the court for Arthur's first volley. Also, when possible, he would chip low to Jimmy's forehand, forcing him to hit up.

I couldn't believe my eyes when Arthur worked his game plan to perfection, winning the first two sets, 6–1, 6–1. But when Jimmy clawed back to take the third set 7–5, I cringed, and Arthur's lead looked like a house of cards ready to topple. Somehow, Arthur kept his cool, winning the fourth set 6–4.

I felt so happy it was as though *I* had won Wimbledon. If my partner could do it, then maybe I could dream as well. Since I had reached the Wimbledon semifinals before I turned 24, I figured there would be more chances to come.

1977 Australian Open

The problem with the Australian Open—the last Grand Slam tournament of the season—was that, until 1987, the Australian Lawn Tennis Association scheduled the tournament for the last two weeks of the year. Beginning in 1987 the Australian Open tournament committee moved the tournament to late January, positioning it as the *first* Grand Slam of the year (which is why no Australian Open was staged in 1986). But before the change, play began before Christmas Day—the height of summer Down Under—and the men's finals often coincided with New Year's Day.

Many top pros didn't want to be anywhere near a tennis court over the Christmas holidays. In addition, Australia's isolation—a 20-hour flight from LAX alone—conspired to keep players near hearth and home. Bjorn Borg and Jimmy Connors, after playing the Australian early in their careers, crossed the tournament off their calendars. Many of the top 10 were no-shows as well.

By the midseventies, the Australian Open had the look and feel of a nationals-only tournament. Indeed, all eight quarterfinalists in 1976 (which was actually played in late December 1975) were Australians because of the diluted field.

Arthur convinced me that we should go to Australia in late 1976. "You or I could win this thing," he predicted. Arthur was a former champion, having captured the Australian the first time he played it in 1970. He had returned a year later and reached the finals, but he had not played the Australian since 1971. I had *never* traveled to Australia or played in the Australian Open, so this would be a first for me. The more I thought about it, though, the more I believed Arthur was right: I *did* have a good chance to win, since the tournament was played on grass. Besides, the Australian Open was still a major, even if not all the top players were there.

The Australian Open back in the seventies was staged on the outskirts of Melbourne on grass courts that the Australians would call "sketchy." Aussie grass was hard as a rock and bumpy compared to Wimbledon's lush courts, where the grass was firm but true—except for Court 2, the "graveyard" court.

Arthur, who was bothered by a bone spur in his right foot, lost in the quarterfinals to John Alexander of Australia. Meanwhile, my march through the draw was like playing a Who's Who of the Australian Tennis Hall of Fame. In the round of 16, I beat Tony Roche. In the quarters, it was Phil Dent (father of American player Taylor Dent). In the semis, I defeated Ken Rosewall, the 42-year-old ageless wonder.

Awaiting me in the final was Guillermo Vilas, the stocky Argentine with long chestnut hair that flowed past his shoulders. He loaded his ground strokes with massive amounts of topspin and sought to win wars of attrition from the baseline. Little did we know that he was about to embark on one of the great years in the Open era. During the 1977 calendar year, Vilas played an unbelievable 159 matches, winning 145. He won two Grand Slams—the French Open and the U.S. Open—and set a Joe DiMaggio–like streak by winning 50 consecutive matches, a mark that may never be beaten. Vilas would go on to win 17 tournaments in 1977.

Of course, neither Guillermo nor I knew what the future held. All I was aware of was Vilas' *past*, and the record book said that he had won the Masters, the ATP's big end-of-the-year tournament, on Kooyong's center court in 1974. I was also aware that Guillermo was coached by Ion Tiriac, the chain-smoking Romanian rascal who was no longer in Nastase's corner. What Tiriac didn't know was that *I* too had a coach for our final-round match on a hot New Year's Day, January 1, 1977.

What happened is that Arthur, who was working on a coffee-table picture book containing his photos, had secured a photographer's pass for the finals. My doubles partner put on a bucket hat and rubbed shoulders with a couple of dozen photographers lying down courtside. During changeovers, he would maneuver himself so that he was behind my chair. With my back turned to him, I heard Arthur whisper advice such as "Serve to his forehand" or "Chip and charge on the next break point."

How could I lose? I was being coached by a great grass-court player, and I responded by playing my best match ever under big-match conditions. I defeated Guillermo easily, 6–3, 6–3, 6–3, and lifted the champion's trophy above my head.

Too bad this would turn out to be my only Grand Slam singles title, but at least I'm an answer to a trivia question: When was the last time a Grand Slam tournament had two champions in the same calendar year? The answer is 1977. I won the Australian on the first day of the year, and Vitas Gerulaitis won the Australian on the last day of 1977 on the Kooyong grass.

1978 Palm Springs

I won 16 professional tournaments, was runner-up 24 times, and captured 13 career doubles titles. But probably the most satisfying victory was the time I whipped Mexico's Raul Ramirez in the finals of Palm Springs.

I *hated* playing Raul Ramirez. He was my college rival when I was at Stanford and he played for USC. He would feed me soft balls that forced me to generate speed, and then he'd take the offense by chipping and charging. I didn't lob all that well, so it was hard for me to get by him because he was a quick, instinctive volleyer (and part of the No. 1–ranked doubles team with my old Baylor school chum, Brian Gottfried).

Another aspect of Raul's game drove me crazy. He had a subtle way of intimidating linesmen and lineswomen by giving them a quick look just as they were about to make their call. Players know that if you keep "registering" on linesmen, lots of time you'll get them to call the ball out, especially on a big point. Whenever Raul influenced a linesman's decision, that made Short Fuse mad.

One year we were playing in Caracas, and I decided I would mimic everything that Raul did. All the guys came out of the locker room to watch me stare down linesmen with bug eyes and an erect gait. A few months later we were having an end-of-the-WCT-season party in Denver, and the players got together to hand out some joke awards. I received the award for Best Acting Job.

We also had a Mishit Award for the player who mishit the most balls on the tour, and the early voting went toward Rod Laver. The Australians said that was sacrilege; you cannot give Rod Laver a Mishit Award, which happened to be a big oar. (We had gone to a sporting goods store and purchased a wooden paddle since the winner always hit it off the wood.) So we decided to call it the Rod Laver Award, and we gave it to Bjorn Borg because he mishit a lot of balls that always went in, and believe me, that was annoying.

When Raul and I marched into the finals of Palm Springs, which in 1978 was held at Mission Hills in Rancho Mirage, I was super-charged to play him. First of all, this was my hometown tournament, since Nancy and I lived next door in Palm Springs. I trained at Mission Hills with my coach, Dennis Ralston, so I had played on the stadium court hundreds of times.

I wanted to beat Raul in the worst way. I bashed my serve as hard as I could, and I remember hitting one at his body that nearly put a hole through his chest. Every stroke of the racket turned into pure gold: I won the first 16 points in a row to grab a 4–0 lead. Playing "in the zone" allowed me to cruise in from there, winning in straight sets. Raul never got a chance to register on a linesman.

After the match, several guys from *Tennis* magazine found me in the locker room. They had some news they wanted to share with me. Apparently, they had brought a radar gun to the match and clocked my serve from the grandstands behind the baseline. (Speed guns on court were not widely introduced until the nineties.)

"We clocked you for speeding," one joked.

"How fast did you get me for?" I asked. I knew I had a big serving day, but I wasn't sure *how* fast.

"One hundred and fifty-three miles per hour."

I let out a low whistle. "I guess I was pretty keyed up out there."

"I'll say you were."

I am well aware that I had a big serve, a weapon that I could use to hurt people—including Raul Ramirez. One time, after I had beaten

Brian Gottfried in a final, he told the crowd, "I can't talk too well. If you had that thing coming at you for three sets, you'd be a little shell-shocked too." That's because Brian had roughly one-fifth of a second from the time the ball left my strings to the time it bounced to react to my serve—the time it takes to stick out your tongue.

The secret to my serve was not how hard I hit the ball but *when* I hit it. My racket connected with the ball as the toss arrived at the top, which was different from when most other players hit the serve—*after* the toss had started down. This meant I was hitting the ball sooner than my opponent expected, and unless he was absolutely ready, my serve was hitting the backstop before he had a chance to put the racket on the ball.

When my serve was on, it was virtually unreadable. One time when I played Jimmy Connors at Wimbledon, I blasted several aces by him. On my next serve, he lifted his hand to stop me. Then I watched as he made a show of shuffling back 10, 15 steps behind the baseline until he nearly sat in a lineswoman's lap. He cupped his right hand around his mouth like he was six furlongs from me. "I'm ready now," he yelled out, and we all enjoyed a laugh.

My fellow pros voted me as having the best serve several years running in the late seventies, and I was proof that you didn't have to be 6'6" with washboard abs and buns of steel to have a devastating serve. Because I was 6' and weighed a slight 170 pounds, I did not cut an imposing figure on the court. I just happened to be blessed with a motion of compactness, having spent many hours on the practice court working the arm and shoulder in unison, hitting cones placed in corners of the service box. Another drill came from Pancho Gonzalez, who once advised me to practice hitting my serves long because in a match I would generally serve shorter.

One thing I didn't have to practice was being left-handed, a huge advantage on the tennis court. Not only are right-handers not used to our spin, which arrives in the opposite way, but also I could hook the serve wide when serving to the ad court. That really helped me get out of jams on break point or win those decisive game points.

So how fast was I? Curry Kirkpatrick of *Sports Illustrated* once wrote that I possessed a "999 mph serve," but the most I ever registered was the unofficial 153 miles per hour in the Ramirez match. That number was eclipsed by Andy Roddick at a Davis Cup match in 2004, when he blazed in a 155-mile-per-hour missile.

So, how has the technology of speed guns changed in 25 years? Were the speed guns of my day accurate? I don't have those answers, but even today there is disagreement about the accuracy of speed guns made by different manufacturers. L. Jon Wertheim, *Sports Illustrated*'s tennis writer, said after a Roddick 153-mile-per-hour bomb in London that serve clockings have become "about as dubious as WNBA attendance figures" because tournaments don't use the same speed gun.

I would think that the computer-aided technology of today's tennis rackets would increase service speed, but when Australian player Mark Philippoussis did an on-court test using his racket and a wooden racket, he only served one mile per hour faster with his modern racket. As for who was the fastest server ever, I'll let tennis historians bat that one around for a while. All I know is that I belong on the same bench as Andy Roddick, Pancho Gonzalez, Greg Rusedski, Pete Sampras, Mark Philippoussis, and Colin Dibley.

1979 Wimbledon

If one match defines a career, then Borg versus Tanner in the 1979 Wimbledon finals is the one I will be remembered for. The fact that I played a memorable match at Wimbledon—the first "Breakfast at Wimbledon" broadcast by NBC—is something I will treasure until I draw my last breath. If that match becomes my epitaph, then I'm perfectly fine with that.

From the time I swatted leaves off the trees next to Mr. Evert's tennis court, I listened to my first tennis coach talk about this magical place called Wimbledon. My young imagination soared. Famed Centre Court with the Royal Box. Lawns lined with chalk and wooden net posts. Strawberries and cream. Players flinging their rackets into the air after they won a Wimbledon title. The Duke and Duchess of Kent making small talk as they handed the winner the coveted Wimbledon trophy.

When I turned pro, I thought of Wimbledon as *the* tournament, the biggest one on my calendar, so I pointed all year to the fortnight at the All-England Club. I put Wimbledon down first on my schedule and worked everything else around it.

I certainly placed an anvil of expectations on my serving shoulder. I expected to do well at Wimbledon because the slick grass-court surface suited my game. All I had to do was hammer my serve into the corners and wait for an opening to break serve.

It sounds so easy to write those words, but the reality is that all it takes is one tentative volley, one butchered overhead, or one key double fault, and you're gone. In 1974, Ken Rosewall stopped me on his run to the finals, where Connors cleaned his clock. I've already mentioned how I had the wrong game plan against Jimbo in the 1975 semifinals.

In 1976, I advanced to the semifinals again, but waiting across the net was Bjorn Borg. Who knows what directions our careers might have taken had I won that match, but after he whipped me in straight sets, he shot off toward immortality by defeating Ilie Nastase for the first of five consecutive Wimbledon titles.

I really thought 1977 would be my year. I was brimming with confidence after winning my first Grand Slam title at the Australian Open in January. I looked at my draw, saw that I was seeded fourth, and charted my way to the semifinals, where Borg would be waiting for me. When an overconfident player does that—looks ahead—he can be humbled, and that's exactly what happened. John Lloyd, a promising player from Great Britain (and future husband of Chris Evert), took me out in the very first round. Then, in 1978, an old nemesis, Ilie Nastase, beat me in the round of 16.

So it was with fresh determination that I trained for Wimbledon in the spring of 1979. England was experiencing a heat wave, which meant the grass courts were baked to perfection. I defeated Van Winitsky, Peter McNamara, Ross Case, and Jose-Luis Clerc out in the "country"—the outer courts—before being invited into Centre Court for my match against Tim Gullikson in the quarterfinals.

While I was working my way to a four-set win, I could hear *singing* from Court 3, where Adriano Panatta of Italy was locked in a duel with Pat DuPre, who played at Stanford the year I turned pro. At that time, England had more Italian waiters per capita than anywhere else in the world, including Rome, and they must have all descended upon Wimbledon that day to cheer on their favorite son. They sang songs during changeovers, went crazy whenever Panatta won a point, and did their best to rattle the young American. I don't know how DuPre came back from being down two sets to one, but he did, setting up a semifinal match between us.

I couldn't believe my luck. Patrick was an unseeded player who had never advanced this far in a Grand Slam tournament, a Cinderella player who had to be wondering when the carriage would turn into a pumpkin. But I wasn't going to look past Pat, whom I had never played before. My motto was "Remember John Lloyd."

I dispatched him in straight sets, and waiting for me was the "Angelic Assassin," Bjorn Borg. Wearing long dishwater-blond hair tucked behind a headband, a scraggly beard, and a stylish pinstripe Fila shirt and shorts, the "stoic Swede," as he was described in breathless news coverage, was said to be so calm that he had a resting pulse of 35 beats per minute. British schoolgirls shrieked whenever they spotted the shy player with the flowing locks and broad swimmer's shoulders. Kiosks all over England sold Bjorn Borg chocolate bars, which were guaranteed not to melt under hot conditions. That was a fit metaphor because some of tennis' biggest names melted under the pressure of the Swede's sizzling ground strokes.

Borg preferred to camp out on the baseline and drive the ball with heavy topspin off both wings. He whacked his forehand with an off-the-handle Western grip and knocked the fuzz off the ball with a two-fisted backhand. He didn't like playing the front part of the court because volleying demanded a severe grip change from his Western grip. The guys in the Wimbledon locker room used to say that Borg's volley was so bad that it was good. Why? Because his short, tentative volleys—which would have sat up on clay or a hard court for an easy put-away—were perfect for Wimbledon's grass courts. The ball didn't bounce well on grass.

The press, though, thought Borg walked on water. As he advanced through the draw, London's Fleet Street scribes employed words like *invincible, formidable, unconquerable,* and *insurmountable*—and that was *before* he destroyed Jimmy Connors in his semifinal match, 6–2, 6–3, 6–2. Minutes after shaking Borg's hand, Connors ran for the limousine to get a ride back to his hotel.

"Can you spare a couple of minutes to talk?" one reporter asked him.

"The minutes are passing," Jimbo said, as he slammed the door and the limo took off.

I knew the press wanted to pepper me with questions after I beat DuPre. I took a shower and sat for a moment in the Wimbledon locker room with my coach, Dennis Ralston, who had some advice for my postmatch press conference.

"I want you to be calm when you walk in there," Dennis directed. "They're going to tell you that you can't beat him, that you have no chance, so you have to be ready for that."

"I don't think Bjorn is invincible," I replied. "I beat him last year at the U.S. Indoors in Philly."

"You and I know that, but try telling that to the press," Dennis said, clearly as exasperated as I was.

"Watch this," I said, as I stood up to leave for the press conference.

I walked into a wood-paneled room downstairs under the players' locker room, where probably 50 members of the media were waiting for me. I sat down at a table, looked around, and immediately felt like I had been tossed into a lion's den. A crescendo of voices shouted questions at me, each taking the story line that Dennis had predicted.

"Do you actually think you can stop Borg?"

"How does it feel to play someone who hasn't lost in four years at Wimbledon?"

"Do you think you have any sort of chance against a great player like Bjorn Borg?"

I held up the palm of my left hand. "Gentlemen, I have an announcement to make before I will answer any questions."

My statement startled the assembled press, who hushed up and found their seats.

"I want you to know that I agree with you guys. I cannot beat Bjorn Borg, so I'm going home. I'm going to default to him."

For a moment, the silence was deafening. While I'm sure a few journalists thought I was pulling their legs, most believed me, which prompted a fresh set of questions.

"Did you say that you're going to default the finals of Wimbledon?" shouted one writer above the din.

"Yes, I did. I've told you guys that if I cannot win, I quit. There's no point in waiting around two more days. Why go out there and embarrass myself on Centre Court? So I'm going home."

"But if you serve well and volley well, wouldn't that give you a chance?" one scribe asked, clearly concerned that I might actually default to Borg.

"Yeah, you have a big serve, Roscoe," another writer agreed.

"I know, but—" I began.

"Borg doesn't like big servers because he doesn't get any rhythm against them," a writer interrupted.

"Really?" I asked. "So if I serve well, I might have a chance?"

A few heads nodded.

"That does it. You guys convinced me to stay. I'll play Borg after all."

After warming up with Dennis on Saturday morning, we walked back to the locker room, which was known at the All-England Lawn Tennis Club as Gentlemen's Dressing Room No. 1. This well-appointed locker room—which looked like something out of the film *Chariots of Fire*—was reserved for tennis royalty: seeded players, former champions, and players whom the All-England committee thought well of. All other players were shuttled off to Gentlemen's Dressing Room No. 2, which wasn't nearly as nice. The English class system really let you know where you stood in the pecking order.

I had a couple of hours to kill before the match, which was set to start at 2:00 *precisely*. Centre Court matches *always* started at 2:00 on the dot; that had been a Wimbledon tradition since the men played in boaters and cream-colored long pants.

I sat down on a pine bench in front of my locker. A pensive Bjorn was seated beside me, trying to relax.

"Mail call."

I looked up, and one of the locker-room attendants was carrying two gunnysacks filled with mail. "This one's for you, Mr. Borg," he said, setting the heavier one next to Borg's feet. "And you have some mail, Mr. Tanner." My mailbag looked to be much smaller, but I understood why. Bjorn's long locks drove the girls crazy, while my hair—curled in a tight perm—must have not quite done it for them. Plus, Bjorn was a bachelor, and I had been married to Nancy for six years.

I thanked the attendant, and for the next half hour, Bjorn and I sat next to each other opening letters, the majority of them wishing us good luck in the finals. Our coaches, Dennis for me and Lennart Bergelin for Bjorn, opened a few to pass the time.

Donald Dell, my agent, dropped by to wish me luck. He motioned me to a quiet corner of the locker room. "There's something you have to do, Roscoe," he said, suddenly looking serious.

"What's that?"

"We've got to find a way to delay this match."

I looked at him like he had sprouted horns. "Donald, what are you talking about? I've played a career to get to this final. I can get penalized for delaying a match. That would be a big problem."

"Listen, NBC has the problem. The link to the satellite doesn't start until 2:00 P.M., but they need to do a lead-in, go to a commercial, and come back before showing the first point."

"Whoa, wait a minute here. You're telling me that you want me to delay the match so they can do their little lead-in and commercial break? NBC is way bigger than me. Let them deal with Wimbledon."

"They tried. You know about the starched collars at the All-England Club: *Play starts precisely at 2:00* and all that balderdash. They think the sun will set on the British Empire if they start after 2:00 P.M."

I knew what Donald meant there. When the Rolex clock on Centre Court hit 2:00, Wimbledon officials wanted the first serve in the air. That meant we had to walk onto the court at eight minutes before the hour so that we had enough time to bow to the Royal Box, spin the racket to see who served, and knock the ball around for five minutes to get loose.

"Well, there's nothing little old me can do," I said.

"I understand," Donald said as he stood up. "I just thought I'd give it a try."

Donald wished me luck again and departed. My agent, who had been commentating on televised tennis matches with Bud Collins since the early seventies on PBS, would be in the broadcast booth with Bud to call my match for NBC's first *Breakfast at Wimbledon*. It is remarkable that NBC allowed this conspicuous conflict of interest, but this was in the early years of televised tennis and Donald knew his stuff behind the microphone.

Prior to 1979, Wimbledon was shown on a delayed basis in the United States—five or six hours after the fact. Even in those pre-Internet days, most tennis fans had already heard the results on the radio. Watching a sporting event when you already knew the outcome did not make for compelling, edge-of-your-seat viewing. Think about it: Arthur Ashe's stunning victory over Jimmy Connors in 1975 wasn't quite so stunning when you knew it would happen.

Then Don Ohlmeyer, NBC's executive producer for sports, had a revolutionary idea: *show Wimbledon live!* Now there was a concept. That meant a 9:00 A.M. start on the East Coast and an awfully early 6:00 A.M. start for West Coast viewers. This was a radical concept because 24-hour sports programming didn't exist (ESPN began Labor Day weekend in 1979), and televised sporting events were found only on the big three networks—ABC, CBS, and NBC—plus a few independent channels. Cable TV was only avail-able in a few parts of the country.

Ohlmeyer had to win over the NBC programmers, who said that the only people watching Saturday morning TV were kiddies catch-ing their favorite cartoons. Ohlmeyer eventually brought any internal doubters around to his point of view, and then an aide came up with a catchy marketing slogan—"Breakfast at Wimbledon."

I'm sure that Ohlmeyer was disappointed to find me on the other side of the net from Bjorn Borg for the inaugural "Breakfast at Wimbledon" broadcast. He was probably hoping that the brash John McEnroe, who had left Stanford after winning the NCAAs the year before, would get through the draw, but that didn't happen. No one was giving me a chance, and London bookies had installed Borg as an 8–1 favorite. I didn't find this out until years later, but when Don Ohlmeyer asked Donald Dell how his client would do, my agent responded, "He'll probably lose one, one, and one."

I sat next to my locker, watching the minutes tick by. Then an idea came to mind, an idea that could delay the match. The more I thought about what I could do, the more I believed I could pull it off.

Before any big match, the tournament keeps the players on hold in the locker room until the appointed time. I knew that around 12 minutes before 2:00, Leo Turner, a locker-room attendant who had probably witnessed the first championships in 1877, would come for our racket bags. That was another Wimbledon tradition: the diminutive Leo, dressed in a white laboratory coat, following us onto Centre Court with our racket bags, where we turned and bowed to the Royal Box. Wimbledon stopped the quaint tradition of bowing and curtseying in 2003, but I always thought that was something unique about this tournament.

Sure enough, Leo arrived right on schedule. "Peter's ready to take you," he said, referring to Peter Morgan, the Wimbledon official who would officially usher us from the locker room to Centre Court and a worldwide audience of tens, if not hundreds, of millions.

I clutched my midsection and groaned. "Oh, Leo, I've got to go to the bathroom."

"Are you all right, my dear boy?" A look of genuine concern came across Leo's face.

"Sorry. It must be the nerves—ooohhh."

Leo accompanied me to the men's loo, which was nearby. I walked into a stall, closed it, and locked the door. Leo left to give me some privacy, but not before I let out another deep groan.

I sat down—fully clothed—on the toilet and looked at my watch.

The seconds slowly ticked by. Three or four minutes later, an anxious Leo barged in. "Mr. Tahn-ner, Mr. Tahn-ner, we've gaht to go," he said in his Cockney lilt. "Mr. Borg is waiting."

I let out a deep moan. "Leo, I can't. I feel sooo sick."

I heard frantic footsteps as Leo left, presumably to tell Peter Morgan that one of his finalists was answering a nasty call from nature.

I looked down at my watch. A few more minutes passed, and then I saw the time: two minutes before 2:00 P.M. I had stalled my entrance by at least eight minutes, and I figured that should give NBC enough time to do their intro and get to their first commercial. *Donald will be so proud of me . . .*

"Mr. Tahn-ner, Mr. Tahn-ner, are you—?"

"I'm feeling a lot better, Leo," I said, as I flushed the toilet. "Sorry about that."

Leo quickly led me to Peter Morgan, who looked a bit exasperated. We still had to follow Wimbledon protocol, which meant leading Bjorn and me to the Players Waiting Room behind Centre Court, where Wimbledon officials would make sure that those seated in the Royal Box were ready for our entrance.

I had seen this room before—two days before, in a movie called *Players* that had just been released. The film was about an aspiring professional tennis player, played by Dino Martin (the son of entertainer Dean Martin), falling in love with Ali MacGraw. Dino was a good player who had played some pro tennis and was ranked in the world's top 200. The backdrop was Wimbledon, and there was a scene in the movie where Dino was about to play Guillermo Vilas in the Wimbledon final (I told you this was a Hollywood movie). The players were shown sitting in the Players Waiting Room, waiting to walk onto Centre Court. Talk about art imitating life. The players looked up to a clock on the wall, and the camera showed a tight shot of the clock about to turn 2:00 P.M.—a drama-building device I suppose. As my eyes scanned the waiting room, I couldn't find the same clock.

"The clock's not here," I said to Bjorn.

"You're right," he said. We had talked in the locker room about the movie, which he had seen as well.

"Follow me, gentlemen," Peter Morgan said, and we followed him onto Centre Court.

I remember being stopped a few steps before the large umpire's stand, which was the signal for Bjorn and me to turn and bow in the direction of the Royal Box. As I respectfully dipped from the waist, I felt the weight of the moment come over me. *Uh-oh, Roscoe, this is history you're making. One way or another, people are going to remember this match.* My greatest fear that day was playing poorly and losing 6–1, 6–1, 6–1, just like my agent had predicted. Better to have lost in the semis than have people remember you for falling on your face in tennis' most prestigious tournament.

Meanwhile, back in the United States, millions of viewers were watching a youthful Dick Enberg, wearing a red jacket, introduce the telecast:

> Centre Court. Historic Wimbledon. The birthplace of championship tennis. Live, for the first time ever, NBC presents the men's finals. Champion Bjorn Borg of Sweden against the No. 5 seed, Roscoe Tanner of the United States. It's a day for tennis historians. Borg is aiming for his fourth consecutive championship here on the lawns of the All-England Club. No man in the modern era has ever accomplished that feat. We had a little rain about an hour ago, but as you can see live, Tanner and Borg are warming up on Centre Court. Fifteen thousand fans are jammed into the World Series of tennis; it's the Kentucky Derby, Masters golf. Wimbledon, 102nd edition. Let's go to Centre Court with Bud Collins and Donald Dell.

I got out all my butterflies during the warm-up. I sensed that Bjorn was nervous, so I applied pressure from the opening game. I knew I couldn't stay back trading ground strokes with him, so I chipped and charged frequently to make him pass me. My serve held up, and I relaxed. In many ways, I was having the time of my life out there on Centre Court. One time, Bjorn and I exchanged rapid-fire volleys at each other, but I lost the point. I playfully slid my racket along the ground with a loud laugh.

We held serve throughout the first set. I scored a lead at 6–4 in the tiebreaker. Bjorn swatted a forehand approach deep into my backhand corner, and on the dead run I flicked a topspin lob off my backhand. I know I shocked Bjorn because I had never hit one in a match, but Dennis and I had been working on a topspin lob off the backhand in practice. All Bjorn could do was take two steps back and helplessly watch the ball drop into the backcourt.

First set, Tanner. I looked up to the Friends Box, where Nancy, Dad, and Dennis were sitting. Unfortunately, at that time players were allowed only three seats in the Friends Box, which meant that Mom had to sit several rows behind. My eyes searched and found Dennis, and I could tell he was in a state of shock after I hit that topspin lob. But I know what the rest of the tennis world was thinking: *At least this match will go four sets.*

I thought I could win this match, even after Bjorn pinned a 6–1 set on me to even up the match. I got an early break in the third and made it stand up. Now I was up two sets to one, and I know what the rest of the tennis world was thinking: *At least this match will go five sets.*

Not me. I was so excited thinking I could actually win Wimbledon that I forgot to play the fourth set. The only good news was that I was serving first in the fifth. I saved a break point at 15–40 with an ace, but Bjorn passed me with a backhand for the break. I trailed throughout the fifth set, but I was constantly putting pressure on his serve. At 4–3 for Bjorn, I had him down 15–40. Break serve, and I would be serving at 4–4 with tons of momentum. Hold my serve, and all the pressure would be on Bjorn's shoulders.

At 15–40, Bjorn served and volleyed, but I hit a great return low to his feet. He popped up a volley to the middle of the court just past the service line, the ball sitting up like it was on a tee. Everything was in my favor: I had a forehand and I had Bjorn up at the net, not at the baseline, right where I wanted him.

I knew Bjorn would cover the crosscourt, so I held my swing a fraction of a second to give him time to get all the way over to the sideline. Sure enough, he shot over there like he was on rocket skids; he was nearly in the doubles court when I fired away. All I had to do was hit the ball anywhere in the vacated court, but when I looked up, my well-struck forehand landed two inches outside the sideline.

"Out!" the linesman yelled. I tried to shake it off. On my next break point, I got to the net first, but I knew my approach wasn't deep enough. Bjorn hit a dipping passing shot that was too much for me to keep in play. At deuce, he struck a nervous approach to my forehand, which I struck well and passed him. I saw a puff of chalk come up as the ball hit the baseline, but the ball was called out. *Oh, what might have been.* I made a mild appeal to the chair umpire, but he stuck with the call. Then Bjorn threaded another winner past me to go up 5–3.

I knew I wasn't done yet. I held serve, but on his service game, he quickly moved to 40–love, triple match point. I remember taking my time and saying to myself, *OK, Roscoe, this is it. There's no more. You might as well leave everything on the table. Go for every one of your shots.*

We got into long baseline exchanges, but I fought him off with two volley winners and a go-for-broke backhand up the line. Bedlam at Centre Court! Borg, up 40–love, triple match point, looked shell-shocked. He would later say, "I could hardly hold the racket. If Roscoe had won that game, there was no way I could win the match."

I agree. Bjorn looked *very* shaky to me, especially after he missed his first serve at deuce. I dumped his second serve into the net, however, trying to come over the backhand.

On his fourth match point, Bjorn and I got into a long baseline rally before I yanked a backhand sideways. My heart sank because victory had been just a few points from my grasp. I watched Bjorn fall to his knees—his trademark expression at Wimbledon—as cameras clicked and the fifteen thousand fans at Centre Court cheered the popular winner.

I didn't feel bad about losing. Just the opposite. I felt ecstatic that I had come within a couple of inches of toppling the Wimbledon champion. I had played a good match. I could hold my head high.

Every year, Bud Collins waits behind Centre Court to interview the players after the match, so I knew that when I turned the corner, Bud and his NBC blazer and loud trousers would be waiting for me.

I thought he asked me the silliest question. "Did you ever think you had a chance?" he queried.

What do you mean? I just lost in five sets. Of course I had a chance. Maybe he asked the question based on what I had said at the press conference after my semifinals match. I don't remember what I said to Bud that afternoon, but I tried to do my best not to make a fool of myself. After all, this was live TV before millions of people.

I was escorted off the court to my stall inside Dressing Room No. 1. There were all sorts of people and lots of commotion going on, and then Leo approached me. In typical British understatement and reserve, he said, "Mr. Tahn-er, would you take a phone call from the president of the United States?"

"Sure, Leo." What else was I going to say?

"If you will follow me, sir." Leo led me into the Wimbledon office, where I was directed to take the phone.

"Hello?"

A voice came on the line. "Mr. Tanner, would you mind holding the line for the president of the United States?"

Just hearing that question caused my heart to skip a beat. "Of course, I'll hold."

The next thing I heard was another voice on the line. "Hi, Roscoe, this is Jimmy Carter."

"Thank you for calling, Mr. President."

"Roscoe, I'm sitting here with the cabinet at Camp David, working on the energy crisis. We thought we would take a break and watch your tennis match."

"I hope you're having better luck than I did, Mr. President."

"We're trying, but I want you to know that you represented the United States very, very well today, and we're proud of you."

"Thank you, sir."

President Carter said something about having to run back into a meeting, but he was glad that he caught me. I thanked him for the thoughtful phone call and hung up, pretty much blown away that the president of the United States would go to the trouble to phone a tennis player from Lookout Mountain, Tennessee, and congratulate him for playing a good match.

I received lots of pats on the back following the Borg match, even from the skeptical media. Wrote Curry Kirkpatrick in *Sports Illustrated*, "In fact, if it had not been for the oppressive, pounding service and otherwise splendid all-around effort of Roscoe Tanner in the final last Saturday, Wimbledon 1979 might have passed into history as the most tedious fortnight ever."

Little did I know that within two months, I would experience the highest of my highs and the lowest of my lows on the tennis court within *two days* of each other.

8

Transition Game

When the U.S. Open moved from Forest Hills to the National Tennis Center at Flushing Meadow in 1978, the USTA continued scheduling night sessions (which started in 1975) so they could sell the same seat twice in a day. Slew Hester, the chairman of the Open, said the night sessions were a way to accommodate working people who couldn't get to the matches before 7:00 P.M. He put all the top players on notice that they could expect to play at least once under the lights before "Super Saturday," when the men's semifinals were sandwiched around the women's final.

Lennart Bergelin, Bjorn Borg's coach, called U.S. Open officials before the 1979 tournament seeking an exemption to nighttime play for his player. He explained that Borg didn't see the ball well at night. Twenty-five years ago the lights weren't nearly as good as they are today, and in Bjorn's defense, the ball is harder to pick up under artificial lighting. Tennis matches are decided by split-second timing. But tournament officials responded by saying none of the players saw as well at night as they did during the day. They weren't going to make an exception, not even for the great Bjorn Borg.

The story line going into the 1979 U.S. Open was that Borg was halfway to the Grand Slam, having won the French Open and Wimbledon earlier in the summer. But Borg had never won the

U.S. Open in eight tries, and the press made a big deal about how Flushing Meadow was the only hole in his résumé. His camp responded that the Swede could lose if forced to play under the lights.

Since I had to be the *last* person Borg wanted to play in a night session, you can only imagine what he and Bergelin were thinking after the tournament committee announced that our quarterfinal match would be played during prime time. I imagine that Bjorn felt like he was being led to the guillotine—and I was wearing a black hood—as we marched onto the court that Wednesday night. A bois-terous, capacity crowd of twenty thousand was into the match from the first game.

What Bjorn didn't know was that I didn't like to play under the lights either. I had astigmatism, so I couldn't pick up the ball that well at night. After reading about Bjorn's attitude toward night tennis in the papers, though, I didn't tell a soul about my night-vision problems.

Bjorn played like he wanted to be somewhere else in the first set, which I took easily. His competitive fire rekindled in the second set, which he captured. But I kept pounding away big serves, which blunted his vaunted return game, and I'm sure playing under the lights neutralized his reaction time. As I con-tinued playing an aggressive serve-and-volley game, I built a two-sets-to-one and 5–3 lead in the fourth, with me serving for the match.

Two of the most bizarre incidents happened to me in that game. Picture the scene: it was after midnight, and the animated New York fans were screaming their heads off with each rapid-fire point. Borg's fans, who were in the majority, implored him to make a comeback and keep his Grand Slam quest alive. Other New Yorkers, who love an underdog, were spurring me to get over the hump. These knowledgeable spectators understood how difficult it was to close out a great champion like Borg.

I knew that it wouldn't be easy. At 5–3, deuce, I was thinking, *Two aces, Roscoe. That's all you need.* I made my low ball toss and smashed my first serve as hard as I could—my guess is that the velocity was in the 140s—but the ball smacked the tape . . . and the net collapsed! I had never seen that happen in a match, and I'm sure that was a first for Bjorn as well.

The crowd tittered as we inspected the crumpled net. Several maintenance men ran onto the court and tried to reinstall the net, but they quickly determined that the metal cable running underneath the white tape had blown apart. This net was busted. It took the repair party about 10 minutes to find a replacement net.

I'm sure the fact that my serve had destroyed a net worked on Borg's mind. I heard him muttering under his breath in Swedish to Bergelin, who was seated courtside. After the delay, the chair umpire gave us two minutes to warm up and awarded me two serves. A service winner led me to match point, and I saw Bjorn's broad shoulders slump.

I hit another good serve, which Bjorn managed to keep in play. I punched a backhand volley to the open court, and all Bjorn could manage was a short lob right in my wheelhouse.

Great, I said to myself as I saw the ball floating . . . floating . . . in the nighttime air. Time seemed to stop as the ball hovered toward me. I stepped up and took a giant swing—and watched in horror as the ball shot into the grandstand seats like it was on a zip line. I had juiced a sitter on match point!

Now it was my turn for my shoulders to sag. Although I hit a big serve to bring me to match point again, Bjorn forced me to miss a forehand volley on my second match point. Then he sizzled two forehand passing shots by me for the break.

Not again . . . .

I reminded myself that we were still on serve, and that if we got into a tiebreaker, my serve could carry the day. Don't ask me how, but I kept my composure, and in the fourth-set tiebreaker, I played cool, calm, and collected tennis, winning 7–2 and sending Borg packing. For the Swede, there would be no U.S. Open victory and no trip to Australia to chase the Grand Slam.

I was the talk of the tournament for two days leading up to Super Saturday. Writers nicknamed me "Hurricane Tanner," and commentators talked about my chances to go all the way with Borg out of the tournament. CBS and the tournament committee had to be pleased that four Americans had reached the semifinals: Jimmy Connors, John McEnroe, Vitas Gerulaitis, and myself. The luck of the draw placed Jimbo and Mac on one half, so I only had to get past Vitas, who was lower-ranked than me, to reach my first U.S. Open final and play one of the big boys. I wasn't looking past Vitas, though, because he had beaten me three out of four lifetime meetings. When a reporter asked if I might have a letdown after beating Borg, I said, "Letdown? Not much chance. This is the U.S. Open, not the Chattanooga Open."

Vitas fielded different questions before our match. When the press asked him hypothetically who he'd rather face, a firing squad or my serve on a hard, fast court under the lights, Vitas said that most tennis players would probably choose the firing squad. "They might miss, but Roscoe doesn't," he said.

I'm afraid that I felt like standing before a firing squad after I squandered a two-sets-to-love lead to Gerulaitis. I really thought I had him early in the third set when Vitas foot-faulted, which led to a service break. The colorful New Yorker, who grew up in nearby Queens, lost his cool after dropping serve, firing a ball at the baseline judge—shades of Nastase!—but he struck a female spectator instead. A ruckus ensued, and I thought Vitas had mentally packed it in. Then he started playing better . . . and better . . . and when he prevailed in a tight third-set tiebreaker, 7–5, I knew I had a match on my hands.

I couldn't roll back the tide, and Vitas squashed me, 3–6, 2–6, 7–6, 6–3, 6–3 to hand me probably my most devastating defeat. I really believe that I was ready to beat John McEnroe, who was 20 years old and in his first Grand Slam final, but we'll never know.

Brand Recognition

The only bright side to my semifinal performance was that I was now among the top five players in the world. In endorsement terms, my stock was soaring. Losing to Borg at the first *Breakfast at Wimbledon* and then beating him in a prime-time match at the U.S. Open certainly upped my Q rating, a measure of name recognition.

Average people on the street had heard of me. *Roscoe Tanner? He's that lefty with a big serve.* This explains why during the summer of 1979, my agent, Donald Dell, fielded a flurry of phone calls from companies asking me to lend my name to their product or endorse their company.

Donald was a good negotiator, and he was able to land "guaranteed" endorsement contracts, which was the industry norm back at the time. With a guaranteed contract, the company is obligated to pay a certain sum regardless of your performance on the court. So while I didn't earn any bonuses for doing well, I didn't receive any less if I lost in the early rounds, either. During the tennis boom years, clothing and equipment companies made long-term deals, some of which didn't pan out when players' rankings went into the tank. These days, player contracts and endorsement deals are laden with performance clauses, meaning that the player has to win major tournaments to earn the big endorsement dollars. I had a contract with Sergio Tacchini, the Italian clothing company, to wear their tennis clothes on court. It was a four-year deal that paid me $100,000, $125,000, $150,000, and $175,000 a year. Then I had a contract with PDP, the company that made the racket I played with. I was an investor in PDP with nine other American players, and since we owned the company, my endorsement contract was more modest, but I still received $50,000 a year until PDP was sold to Le Coq Sportif. The French company tore up my old contract and re-signed me for $75,000, which escalated to $100,000 a year.

I also had a contract with Pony shoes for five years, and that was for $50,000 a year with an escalation clause of $25,000 a year. In my final year, I was receiving $125,000 a year. I also had a contract to represent Kiawah Island, a resort island off the coast of South Carolina, as a "touring pro." That paid $15,000 a year, plus the title to a two-bedroom condo.

I mention all these contracts for several reasons. Yes, prize money and endorsement income skyrocketed during the boom years of the seventies. The days of being handed £50 checks at Wimbledon were history. Compared to the pittances that long-suffering pros like Rosewall and Laver received in the late sixties, tennis had made me a wealthy man.

But three points must be made:

1. All the money was stacked at the top. Bjorn Borg and Jimmy Connors, who collected the most titles, scooped up the serious money. When Borg left the game in 1981, he had amassed a fortune estimated to be in the $60 million range. I'm sure Jimmy was in the same ballpark.
2. For pros further down the food chain, the money was very good, if not handsome, but not even close to what Borg and Connors (and probably Vilas) were raking in. I never made more than $400,000 a year in prize money, which wasn't chump change, but not the big bucks.
3. Today's pros make 20 times what we did 25 years ago. To illustrate the difference, after I lost to Borg in the Wimbledon final, my runner-up check was for $22,000. When Andy Roddick lost to Roger Federer on Centre Court in 2004, he received $505,000, a 2,300 percent increase in 25 years!

I received a lot more than money for playing tennis at a world-class level. Payment came in other ways: fame, notoriety, and attention. I loved the red-carpet treatment, not having to wait to be seated at busy restaurants, and free upgrades on the airlines.

Following my career year in 1979, Nancy and I went house-hunting, and we found a beautiful home—OK, it was a mansion—in Montecito just south of Santa Barbara. In a neighborhood filled with luxurious homes on oversized lots with long driveways, we settled into a Spanish villa that set us back $500,000. (Our home was located not far from where Oprah lives, and I heard that it sold in 2004 for $9 million. What might have been . . .)

Nancy and I also settled into a marriage of convenience. She had stopped traveling full-time with me in 1977, and the only time she joined me on the road was for the two majors, Wimbledon and the U.S. Open. While the cat was away, the mice were at play. I had numerous affairs on the road with women willing to be bedded by a famous tennis player. There was that cute young woman in England, the voluptuous bombshell in Brazil, and the beautiful down-to-earth young woman in Colorado. I didn't have a girl waiting for me in every port, but I didn't have trouble finding female companionship for the evening or for the week. I was such a smooth talker that maybe I would have become a good lawyer after all. My charming side said what they wanted to hear so that I could get what I wanted.

On the tennis court, I hated cheating, and that was the last way I wanted to win a match. That's why I gave Nastase that point at the U.S. Open. But away from the court, I cheated on Nancy with abandon. Sure, it wasn't easy the first few times, but eventually I was able to stuff any guilty feelings into deep, deep places within my heart. I justified my actions by telling myself that I didn't like being alone. I needed the comfort of a warm embrace because the tour was a lonely place, where wolves were looking to devour lambs on the court.

I hid these affairs from Nancy. I don't think she suspected anything because we got along well when I was off the tour. During much of my career, I was usually home one week a month, and less during the European season from May until July. I've mentioned that Nancy always joined me for Wimbledon, but I can remember having female company at the players' hotel—the Westbury Hotel in London's West End—before my wife arrived from the States.

As far as I knew, Nancy liked living in Santa Barbara. I don't know what she did with her days, which shows how much I was tuned in to her life. I imagine she liked being home, puttering around the garden and doing things around the house. She had girlfriends whom she spent time with, and her parents didn't live too far away in Fillmore, which was outside of Ventura.

Nancy and I clearly lived in different orbits. However, we were still married, and even *I* understood that should count for something. We definitely didn't want to have children during the early years of our marriage because I would have been an absentee dad, but after the 1979 season, we both knew that I wouldn't be playing that many more years. Very few players have the reflexes to compete at the top levels when they're in their thirties.

When Nancy talked about having a child in early 1980, I thought that might be a good development for our marriage. We stopped using birth control, and when she joined me in London for an indoor tournament that fall, we conceived underneath the covers in Room 16 at the Wilbraham Hotel.

Nancy enjoyed—endured—a normal pregnancy, and I was in the delivery room on July 28, 1981, when Lauren was born in Santa Barbara Cottage Hospital. Like all first-time fathers, I was amazed by the birth process that brought a new life into the world. I remember holding Lauren in her swaddling clothes and kissing her on the cheek.

Nancy loved being a mother, and she transitioned well into that role. Did becoming a father cause me to think that maybe I should grow up a little bit or become a more devoted husband and father? I wish I could answer in the affirmative, but I can't. It wasn't long, perhaps three or four months, before I fell into my old ways, getting caught up in more affairs with women around the world. You see, the most important person in my life was Roscoe Tanner.

Dealing with Pain

I continued to play well in the early eighties, even winning tournaments in Bristol, England; Memphis, Tennessee; Sydney, Australia;

and La Costa outside of San Diego. All those years of snapping serves began taking a toll on my left arm, however, and the post-match aches and pains didn't go away very quickly.

One time, in the summer of 1982, I was playing Peter Fleming and he served wide to my backhand in the deuce court. I stretched to reach the ball, but the serve ricocheted off the end of my racket. That caused a shooting pain in my left elbow, much the way a base-ball player experiences a "stinger" when he fouls a pitch off the end of his bat.

I shrugged off the intense pain, chalking it up as one of the dis-comforts of being a professional tennis player. Complaining was not in my nature. A year or two before, my left foot bothered me to the point where I thought I needed an orthopedic specialist to look me over. He was marveled by the X-ray results. "I would say that you've probably had seven stress fractures over the years," he stated, yet I had been treated for nary a one. I came from the school where you toughed it out and taped it up before going out on the court.

This time, the elbow pain following the Peter Fleming match didn't go away like the foot stress fractures. My left elbow was *killing* me. When the 1982 season ended, I visited a Chattanooga doctor, but he couldn't find anything wrong.

"But, Doc, the pain has been intense," I explained. "It hurts!"

"We can try a cortisone shot," he suggested.

The needle looked like it could be used on a horse, but at that point, I would have let him use a butane torch on my elbow if that would have relieved my pain. The cortisone shot did nothing to ease my discomfort, however. Since I had a ranking to protect and a livelihood to look after, I soldiered on.

At the 1983 Wimbledon, I made another good run, upsetting fifth-seeded Mats Wilander to reach the quarterfinals. My elbow was sore as heck, though. Throughout the fortnight I popped Advil and completely rested my arm on my days off between matches.

Waiting for me in the quarterfinals was Ivan Lendl, the young no-nonsense Czech making a name for himself. He had risen to third in the world behind Connors and McEnroe, but I thought I had the game to beat him on grass.

I was supposed to have the day off before our quarterfinal match while the ladies played their four quarterfinals. Then Don Ohlmeyer and NBC looked at the match-ups and decided they needed a men's match to draw some viewers. The Wimbledon officials contacted me and asked if I would be willing to play on consecutive days.

I don't know why I said yes, but I did. My arm was killing me, and I couldn't summon the big gun like I used to. I lost a close match to Lendl, 7–5, 7–6, 6–3, and as I gathered up my racket bag and left Centre Court, I never thought this would be my last match at Wimbledon, but it was.

Meanwhile, my sore elbow continued to bother me as I nursed it through the rest of my summer and fall tournaments. Toward the end of the year, I sought out Dr. Frank Jobe, a Los Angeles orthopedist who had pioneered the "Tommy John" elbow surgery and resurrected the careers of hundreds of athletes. Dr. Jobe, during his examination, did an interesting thing: he had me lift up my left arm and put it into the "back-scratching" position of the serve, and then he took an X-ray.

The damage could be seen as clear as a windswept day. A piece of bone had broken away in the elbow area, and the cartilage was torn. "I don't know how you combed your hair," Dr. Jobe said.

We scheduled surgery immediately. Dr. Jobe said that if I woke up with an Ace bandage around my elbow, then he and his team of skilled surgeons had operated on me with an arthroscope—a good thing. If, however, I woke up with a cast, then my elbow had been worse than expected, and I could look forward to 10 months of rehab instead of several weeks.

The night before my surgery I did something stupid: I watched the movie *Coma*, which was about athletes who underwent surgery but never woke up again because the doctors harvested their organs. Following the surgery, I opened my eyes in the recovery room, and I remember looking to see if the other guys on gurneys were alive. Whew! No sheets over their heads.

Then I remembered to look at my left arm. No cast!

The rehabilitation program progressed on schedule. Dr. Jobe cleared me to play, but he said that I shouldn't serve hard.

That was like telling a fat person to stick to fruit and veggies in the buffet line, but I went with the program. I signed up to play team tennis in the summer of 1984 with the Los Angeles Strings. Our team was playing in the Forum one night against a team led by Brad Gilbert. Gilbert later coached Andre Agassi for eight years before becoming Andy Roddick's coach for a short time.

Back in 1984, Brad wasn't, shall we say, as mature as he is today. He taunted our girls in the doubles match, hurling needling comments their way to get under their skin. Short Fuse got mad—and vowed to get even. When Brad and I played our singles set, I decided to hit him with a serve. I completely forgot about my tender elbow and cranked one up like the old days. I nutted that serve, and it struck Brad right in the . . . let's just say I hit him where it counts. Brad dropped like he had been shot, and I tasted the warm dish of revenge.

That serve turned out to be cold comfort, however, because my elbow hurt for days and weeks afterward. I was reduced to serving at half pace, just spinning the ball in there to get the point started. I played a few more tournaments that summer leading up to the 1984 U.S. Open, but losing to qualifiers in the first round wasn't doing it for me. After Matt Doyle handily defeated me in the first round of the U.S. Open, I decided to retire and walked away from the game I had loved.

A Different Kind of Court

This period was also the time when I walked away from the woman that I had loved—Nancy. I wanted out of the marriage because I wasn't happy being married to her and because I had this girl in Colorado. Let's call her Jill.

Jill was one of those casual tour relationships that blossomed into a full-blown love affair. In 1983, when I was dealing with elbow problems and wondering if my tennis career was over, Jill and I grew closer. I thought starting over with her would be a good way to transition into the next phase of my life.

After wavering for several months, I pulled the trigger. It happened as I was packing my bags for a tournament in Stuttgart. Nancy was staying behind in Montecito, of course, to care for Lauren, who wasn't quite two years old. I asked her to give me a ride to the Santa Barbara airport.

Just before we hopped in the car, I said, "Nancy, there's something I need to tell you."

"What, Roscoe?" She didn't suspect a thing.

"I want a divorce."

Her eyes welled up, and she began crying. I had hurt her deeply, and I'm sure she was thinking that she had done nothing to deserve this horrible treatment. "No, I don't want a divorce. And Lauren needs a father."

"I think it's the right thing," I said coldly.

That was one frosty car ride to the airport, but during the long flight over the Atlantic, my thoughts turned to Jill, who would be meeting me in Stuttgart. *You'll feel better when you see her,* I thought.

When I returned from Europe, I picked up some clothes and things at the house and moved in with Jerry Hatchett, the head pro at the Knowlwood Tennis Club in Santa Barbara. Jerry, a confirmed bachelor, had become a good buddy of mine.

Jill returned to Colorado following our tryst in Stuttgart. I called her and said I wanted to fly out to Denver to visit her.

"No, now's not a good time," she said.

"I really want to spend some time with you," I said, but she rebuffed me again. That's when I smelled a rat. "Why can't I come to Colorado?" I demanded.

"Ah, I'm just a small-town girl. It would make me nervous if you were here or if you met my friends."

We batted that around for a bit, and then she stunned me with a lightning bolt.

"Roscoe, there's something I have to tell you. I'm pregnant."

Shivers ran down my spine. I thought we had been pretty careful. . . .

"But it's not yours," she added.

Now I was really thrown for a loop, but at least I understood why she didn't want me to come to Colorado. I took a few moments to recover, and then I wished her the best. I quietly hung up the phone and never contacted her again.

There were other fish in the sea, I figured. That fall, Jerry, who loved to dance, said I just had to meet the manager of a disco-type nightclub called Peppers on Santa Barbara's famed State Street. "She's quite a dancer," he said.

I was a horrible dancer, but his proposition sounded like something fun to do. We dropped by Peppers to check out the scene, and then Jerry called over Charlotte Brady, the manager. I found her to be quite nice and quite attractive. She stood 5'2" in high heels and probably weighed 105 pounds. We danced some, talked some, drank some beers, and had a good time. She said she was divorced and raising a 10-year-old son as a single mom. I mentioned that I was separated from my wife. When I asked for her phone number, she didn't hesitate to give it to me.

I liked Charlotte right away. The next day, I called and asked her out. She said yes, and I soon had a new girlfriend.

Love and Roses

My declaration to seek a divorce prompted Nancy to hire a divorce attorney. When Mom got the news, she called to say that she was dead set against me splitting up with Nancy.

"I don't believe in divorce. If you move back to Tennessee with Nancy, we can help you work it out."

I wasn't interested in staying married or working things out. I decided that divorce was what I needed for my happiness. I didn't want to listen to Mom's wise advice. I thought I knew what was best—for me. I let Nancy keep the house in Montecito until we could divide community property. I knew I couldn't sleep in Jerry's extra bedroom for the rest of my life, so I set out to find a place of my own. Then I remembered my association with Kiawah Island, South Carolina. I flew back, took a look at a few condos, and purchased a three-bedroom unit right on the beach. (Nancy and I had sold the previous condo a few years earlier.)

I knew as much about decorating a home as I knew about ironing shirts—nothing. Mom, who had spoken her mind regarding the pending divorce, put her feelings behind her when I asked her to help me furnish my new place. She and Dad flew to Kiawah Island during the week of Mother's Day and helped pick out beds and dressers and sofas and assorted knickknacks at nearby furniture stores. We needed everything, from dishes and cutlery to a washer and dryer.

Mom loved turning a house into a home, and within a week, her touch brought life to what had been an empty unit with bare walls. While we shopped and stocked the kitchen, we discussed my pending divorce. Without Nancy there to present her side, I brought Mom around to my point of view. I told her I wasn't happy being married to Nancy, and I didn't want to go through life miserable. Nancy wasn't happy either, so it would be better for both parties if we had an amicable split. Mom didn't turn cartwheels, but she seemed to grudgingly accept my reasoning. Then again, when given enough time, I was usually able to smooth-talk someone into agreeing with me.

We parted, and I left the next day to play an exhibition tournament in Tulsa, Oklahoma. I had just finished my first-round match when I was told that there was an urgent phone call for me in the tournament office.

Pops has died, I immediately thought. My grandfather had been very ill and hospitalized for the last month with pneumonia.

"Hello?"

"Roscoe? It's your father speaking," the voice croaked. I had never heard my father sound so shaky.

"It's Mom. They couldn't save her. . . ." Then his voice trailed off.

Mom? My mother had been vibrant, full of vim and vigor when I said good-bye to her two days earlier in Kiawah Island.

My world turned numb. She was just 63 years old. She couldn't be dead.

"Wha . . . what happened, Dad?" I managed.

"She was out in her garden—you know she loved her rose bushes," Dad said. "She came into the house and said she felt tired. She lay down and fell asleep, and that's when her heart stopped. I called the paramedics, but they couldn't revive her. The doctor said she experienced no pain."

This just wasn't possible. All through my life, Mom had been there for me. She drove me to school, signed me up for tennis lessons with Mr. Evert, put me into Cub Scouts, and traveled with me to more junior tournaments than I could count. Now she was gone, and I felt as though I had lost an anchor in my life.

Several months after Mom died, Nancy and I squared off in divorce court. This turned out to be a no-holds-barred contest between two sides out to get the other party. Nancy had hired an aggressive legal team to represent her, and I had my own battery of lawyers. There was a discovery phase. Each side took depositions. Witnesses were cross-examined.

Her side presented experts that testified that my name was worth a million dollars. My side said I was at the end of my career, headed for the dustbin of washed-up athletes, who are quickly forgotten by the sporting public. We were fighting over this because most of my guaranteed endorsement contracts with Tacchini, Le Coq Sportif, and Pony were still paying out hefty sums and had several years left on them.

The courtroom became a battle zone. My side wheeled a clothes rack before the judge. About a dozen pairs of nice slacks were hanging on the rack. What happened is that after I left for Stuttgart,

Nancy went into my closet and used a seam ripper to cut out all the crotches of my pants. Then she took a pair of scissors and cut holes in my pockets. When I picked up my clothes, I hadn't noticed her tailoring. I flew to New York with a pair of altered black dress slacks. I put them on and walked downstairs to pick up a cab. That's when I noticed that things were a bit drafty down there. That was a good one; I have to award style points to Nancy for that idea.

But when we wheeled those crotchless slacks into the court-room, Nancy turned as white as a sheet. Advantage Tanner.

Not for long. In tennis terms, Nancy captured a straight-set victory. After five contentious and ugly days in court, the judge granted Nancy a million-dollar settlement, plus the Montecito house, now worth $700,000. As part of that settlement, Nancy received 50 percent of my outstanding contracts, which were valued at $1 million. I was ordered to pay the taxes on the entire $1 million and then pay Nancy her half—$500,000—leaving me with my "half"—around $150,000 after taxes. The court also ordered me to pay $8,000 a month in alimony and $2,000 a month in child support for good measure.

I had taken it in my tennis shorts, so to speak. Over the next few months, I liquidated IRAs (which were counted toward my side by the court) to pay my attorney fees, which amounted to $75,000. I heard that she paid her legal team $100,000, further proof that the only ones who win in divorce court are the attorneys.

A year after the divorce decree, my net worth was around $100,000. If tennis had made me a wealthy man, a contested divorce had taken most of it away, and my big paydays were long gone.

9

Break Point

As I transitioned out of the pro game and signed over most of my money to Nancy, I needed to replenish my bank accounts. Things seemed to fall into place. My agent, Donald Dell, booked me for well-paying speaking engagements and corporate outings organized through *Sports Illustrated*'s speakers' bureau. For a princely five-figure sum, I would fly to a company's event—the employee picnic or the annual shareholder's meeting—and give a clinic. I dispensed pointers and spun a few yarns about playing Borg and Connors, and then I'd invite anyone to face my serve.

Naturally, duffers loved the chance to stand across the net from me and punch their racket at a service missile coming at them at 120-plus miles per hour. At one such corporate outing, a visibly pregnant woman insisted on trying to return my serve. I could see it now: my heat-seeking serve nailing her bulging abdomen and causing her to deliver a stillborn child.

"Tell you what, ma'am," I said. "I don't want you to move at all. As long as you don't move, I can miss you."

I tossed the ball and busted one up the middle, but to my horror, she lunged to her left, and my serve nailed her right in the stomach. Her lack of common sense petrified me, and I feared that I was about to witness my second childbirth. Fortunately, she turned out to be OK, but I vowed never to pull that stunt again.

Besides the corporate outings, I also moved into the broadcasting booth, where I commentated on matches for ESPN and the USA Network. I liked TV work and staying in the public eye. In the TV world, being a smooth talker paid off, and my producers liked my work.

When I wasn't on the road, I preferred living in Santa Barbara instead of the Kiawah Island condo. Charlotte and I had become inseparable, and we married during a ski trip to Lake Tahoe in late 1984, right after my divorce from Nancy. She was four months pregnant at the time of our wedding.

We came back from our honeymoon and moved into her apartment. Our daughter, Tamara, was born April 18, 1985, and after staying home two months to care for her, Charlotte returned to Peppers as a manager.

The nightclub was losing money. A couple of Charlotte's acquaintances talked to me about infusing the nightclub with capital. After Nancy had emptied my pockets (in more ways than one), I didn't have any serious assets hanging around, but I still had an income, and I knew where serious money could be found. I played golf with the president of Santa Barbara Bank & Trust, who was a big tennis fan as well. When the three of us approached him about borrowing $100,000 to invest into Peppers, he said, "Lend money to you guys? No problem." The best part was that we didn't have to put up any collateral.

One of our new partners was a bail bondsman who took an interest in running the club. When I was out of town, he ordered the DJ to play street music, not because he liked it but because he thought that would draw a good crowd.

The opposite happened. We lost our "disco" base, and the street kids who gyrated to their music weren't big spenders at the bar. Peppers began hemorrhaging more money.

One night I was at our home, and I heard a knock on the door.

I answered it, where a well-dressed young man in his early twenties stood on the doorstep.

"I'm here to buy."

"Buy? Buy what?" I had no idea what he was talking about.

"Are you stupid, man? Charlotte lives here, right?"

"Yes, but—"

"She sells to me, man."

"Sells?"

"Coke, man. Are you stupid?"

"Well, she's not here now, so you'll have to come back later."

I closed the door and waited for Charlotte to finish the night shift at Peppers. When she walked in the door, I explained the shocking incident from earlier that evening.

"I'm selling drugs to pay the bills," she said. "You know how things are at the club these days."

"I don't want you selling drugs," I declared righteously. Then an idea came into my head. "Tell you what. I'll buy the drugs from you so that you don't have to sell."

I counted off the correct amount of cash and congratulated myself for doing the chivalrous thing. I became curious. "Do you use this stuff?" I asked.

"I have. You've never tried coke?"

I shook my head. I hadn't done drugs since I tried pot in the Stanford dorms.

"It's an amazing drug," she said.

"Really?" If Charlotte thought it was something good, then maybe . . . "Well, it seems that this is my cocaine. Shall we give it a try?"

Charlotte knew exactly what to do, creating "lines" on a mirror and using a crisp, rolled-up $100 bill to sniff the cocaine. From the first hit, I could tell she wasn't a novice. She had hidden that part of her life from me.

Doing drugs with Charlotte was about the dumbest thing I'd ever done. How could I be so stupid? My entry into the drug lifestyle nearly wrecked me because coke addled my ability to think clearly. When I was sniffing that stuff, I missed corporate appearances, didn't show up for appointments, and generally couldn't be found when people needed me. I burned more than a few bridges.

I wasn't a big druggie, but during the two years I was into drugs, I threw away money on the stupidest things—spur-of-the-moment trips to Hawaii, new furniture, and extravagant ski trips to Beaver Creek in the Rockies. We purchased a million-dollar home in Hope Ranch in Santa Barbara, which gave us a mortgage way beyond what we could afford.

I trusted people I shouldn't have. I tried to do things in business that I had no business trying, like the time I tried to promote my own tennis tournament. I had a great batting average—everything I invested my time, talent, and savings into lost money. Nobody had a worse nose for business than me, but perhaps that's because my nose was into cocaine.

Somehow, Charlotte and I muddled on. We continued spending more than we had and ran up the credit cards. We had a lot of bills because we had become a family of four when Anne joined our clan on July 19, 1990.

I kept my hand in tennis by playing a new seniors tour that Jimmy Connors had started. The 35-and-older tour was populated by the same old guys I had been playing for 20 years: Connors, Gottfried, Vilas, Nastase, and so on. These weekend tournaments offered a chance to win some pin money, but nothing like the purses on the ATP tour.

Too bad there weren't many senior events. It was also too bad that ESPN and the USA Network found new blood for the broadcast booth, but to be honest, tennis commentating didn't pay that much. And it was a bummer that fewer and fewer companies were interested in having me bang serves at their employees. As I looked around for a way to support Charlotte and the kids, I turned to teaching tennis lessons. The money didn't compare to the old days on the tour, but the 40 or 50 bucks an hour I earned helping people with their strokes sure beat bagging groceries for a living.

Then I caught a break. A billionaire, David Murdock, was building arguably the most exclusive golf and tennis club in Southern California. The Sherwood Country Club near Thousand Oaks would offer members grass, clay, and hard courts, as well as a championship golf course. Million-dollar homes would line the fairways. Nobody was more thrilled than I was when I was offered the position of tennis director at a handsome salary.

When Charlotte and I moved the family to Westlake Village, we felt like we were getting a fresh start. All I had to do was keep my nose clean.

A Call Away

A couple of years after joining the Sherwood Country Club, I flew to New York City to play in a seniors doubles event. After finishing my match, I made a beeline back to the hotel, where I knew some of the guys would be waiting for me in the bar, drinking their beers. I looked forward to someone yelling, "It's your shout," just like the old days on the tour.

I downed probably a half dozen glasses of Heineken. I liked getting a buzz on; it helped me escape the worries of our tottering financial condition. After a couple of hours of drinking and telling war stories, I walked back to my hotel room.

I don't know what possessed me to do what I did next. I found the yellow pages and let my fingers do the walking—to the pages marked "Escort Services." I looked at several ads, then contemplated what I should do. I knew escort services were a prostitution front. I was aware that escort girls expected to be asked to do a lot more than accompany a lonely businessman to dinner. Of course, you paid according to what you ordered off the menu.

I had an urge for female company, but let's face it: groupies didn't hang around senior events. I nervously dialed the number and asked for an escort to come to my hotel room.

A half hour later, a woman knocked on the door. She looked pretty, and her olive skin spoke of Italian ancestry. She said her name was Connie.

"Come in," I said.

"Nice place you have here," she said, setting her purse down. "Must be kind of lonely traveling these days."

She was a pro. With that opening, we got down to brass tacks and agreed to a price.

Sometime during the middle of the night, I thanked her for her time. Within days, I forgot about her—just like I had forgotten about all the other one-night stands over the years. That part of my life had to go into a secret compartment.

A couple of months later I received a phone call at the Sherwood Country Club.

"This is Connie Romano," the voice said.

"Who?"

"Connie—your escort at the Waldorf Hotel in New York."

"What are you calling about?" I was irritated. She knew the unwritten rules.

"I'm pregnant."

"So?"

"You are the father."

That declaration sent my mind spinning. "This cannot be true," I mumbled. Then I tried to regain the upper hand. "Even if I am the father, I'll deny having ever met you."

"We have our records," she said. "You can expect to hear from my lawyer."

With that, the phone went dead, and it felt like a shakedown. I later heard from her lawyer, who said he had a way to "make this problem disappear." If I paid Ms. Romano a half million dollars, I

The Stanford tennis team—OK, we looked more like the Stanford band—gathered on the tarmac with coach Dick Gould (second row, far left) before flying off to Hawaii at Christmastime in 1970. We gave some clinics, played a few exhibitions, and sampled a few umbrella drinks. I'm in the first row, second from the right.

I dressed up in a coat and tie to announce that I was turning pro in 1972 and would skip my senior year at Stanford University.

This was my official Association of Tennis Professionals (ATP) mug shot when I joined the pro tour in 1972. Unfortunately, it would not be my last mug shot.

When I turned pro, I joined the World Championship Tennis (WCT) Tour, which played most of its winter and spring tournaments indoors.

Debonair, suave, and sophisticated—that's the image that Hart Schaffner & Marks sought to project when they asked me to model their clothes, as seen here at the Chattanooga Tennis Club, circa 1974.

Have racket, will travel. I played with Progressive Development Program (PDP) rackets in Sergio Tacchini clothes.

I liked serving on the hallowed lawns of Wimbledon, where the slick grass made my first delivery nearly impossible to return. At the first Breakfast at Wimbledon in 1979 (bottom), I lost to Bjorn Borg in five sets. Bottom photo courtesy of John Russell.

Dennis Ralston (inset) was a great coach who helped me reach the top five in the world in 1979. Top photo courtesy of John Russell.

In the late seventies, I went for the permed-hair look. Here I'm competing in Palm Springs in 1979.

This shot also was taken at the Palm Springs tournament, where I had some of my greatest success on the tennis court.

would never hear from her again. If I didn't, she would go public and ruin my reputation.

Now it really felt like a shakedown, but I couldn't approach the police. Questions would be asked. Files would be opened. Prosecutors would get involved. The media would be tipped off.

There was another problem. I didn't have a half million dollars sitting around in a bank account. Truth be told, I was living month to month from my salary and lessons at the Sherwood Country Club.

So I stonewalled. Made myself scarce. Didn't return phone calls.

Connie and her attorney called my bluff. They filed for a judgment against me in Somerset County, New Jersey, but I didn't show up. Charlotte caught wind of what was happening, but I lied to her as well, saying this Connie woman was a gold-digger trying to claim paternity after being knocked up by some other guy.

I consented to taking a DNA test, thinking that would somehow clear me since I had no idea who Connie had been sleeping with. That move backfired when the results came back with a 99.4 percent certainty that I was the father.

Once again, my actions had caused my world to fall down around my ears. I had been through this drill before, and I didn't have the patience for a long, drawn-out legal battle. This time around, I quietly agreed to a $500,000 settlement because I'd been approached by a Los Angeles developer about lending my name to the Roscoe Tanner Tennis Club to be built in the San Fernando Valley. My cut would be $1 million. As for the home front, I managed to convince Charlotte that the test was rigged, which saved my marriage—at least for the short term.

Go East, Young Man

David Murdock, the billionaire behind the Sherwood Country Club, didn't play tennis or golf. He ran Sherwood like a Wall Street corporation, so I found myself in mahogany-paneled boardrooms doodling on a yellow legal pad while the numbers guy talked about retention rates or boosting food and beverage sales. I didn't mind the long meetings; in fact, I was learning the button-down corporate culture, which was a good thing.

In 1994, Mr. Murdock shook things up in the boardroom and hired a new general manager. I was playing Jimmy Connors' senior tour 10 to 15 weeks a year back then, and I think being away from the kitchen so much sealed my fate. The new general manager called me into his office one Monday morning after a seniors tournament and regretfully informed me that Murdock had terminated my contract as director of tennis.

I accepted the news gracefully, especially because there was a severance package to soften the blow, but being let go—OK, fired— by Sherwood Country Club was one more brick atop the back of a wobbly marriage. Charlotte and I argued about a lot of things, but the sorry state of our teetering finances was often at the root of our ugly disagreements. One thing we agreed on, however, was that we were living in one of the most expensive regions of the country and we needed to lower our living expenses in a hurry.

We made a bold move back to Tennessee—Mom would have been impressed—to see if a change of scenery would help our struggling marriage. I was still playing the senior tour, so that was bringing in some money, and IMG (my new management firm after I left ProServ) found me a sweet little job as tennis director at Groves Isle, a resort near Miami's Coconut Grove.

Meanwhile, I was always looking for the next big deal that could bail us out of trouble. Charlotte and I rolled our California equity into a 130-acre wooded property outside of Chattanooga after talking with a new set of "investors" about constructing the Tanner Tennis Lodge, a destination resort. An architect had drawn up plans calling for 140 hotel rooms, a fine dining restaurant, eight outdoor and four indoor tennis courts, a fitness center, a spa, conference rooms, and even a blue-water lake stocked with fish.

I honestly believed the opening of the Tanner Tennis Lodge would erase many of my financial and personal problems because I would be paid $1 million by the investors (sound familiar?) for lending my name to the project. I could cut Connie Romano a check for half a million and use the remaining money to steady our financial boat. According to my court settlement with Ms. Romano, I was also supposed to make monthly child-support payments of $1,500, but even that amount was too much. Every now and then I made a good-faith payment, but after several years, I was in arrears to the tune of $40,000. Once again, I ignored phone calls from her lawyers and didn't even bother opening the letters with a New Jersey return address. If I had, I would have noticed that I had received three summonses to appear in Somerset County Superior Court.

In the spring of 1997, I was playing the Nuveen Masters event in Naples, Florida, with Jimmy Connors, Bjorn Borg, John McEnroe, and the other usual suspects. After losing my singles match, I drove a tournament car back to my hotel room. I had just finished showering when I heard a knock on the door.

Two plainclothes Naples police officers stood in the doorway.

"Mr. Tanner?" one asked.

"Yes?"

"A warrant for your arrest has been issued by the Somerset County Superior Court in New Jersey for failure to appear in court regarding a child support issue. I'm afraid you're going to have to come in with us."

I looked at one cop and then the other. They were *serious.* I knew I couldn't talk my way out of this one, so I grabbed my wallet and let them escort me to the squad car.

Now this was a first—I had never been arrested before. I treated the experience rather cavalierly, thinking, *They can't touch me!* How dumb.

At the station I was informed that bail had been set at $5,000, which sounded like a lot of money until the woman police officer behind the desk informed me that I only had to post $500 to get myself out of jail. Cash, though. I luckily had $500 in my wallet to pay the bail bondsman to get me out, but I didn't get out of jail until the wee hours of the morning.

Again, I treated the whole thing as a lark, and the smirk on my face must have been the reason the fans gave me a standing ovation—the story of my arrest had been front-page news in the *Naples News* sports page—as I walked onto the court for my Friday night doubles match with my partner, Tim Wilkison. The guys in the locker room thought it was pretty funny that one of their own had to spend half the night in the slammer.

The smile would soon be erased from my face. Within a year, my life had crumbled yet again. It turned out that the judge in Somerset County really did want me to pay $500,000 to Ms. Romano. If he had dropped two zeros from the sum, I might have managed, but not half a million. Then my investors in the Tanner Tennis Lodge weren't coming though. I kept hoping that the deal would go through, but the financial pressure became too great, and my personal finances toppled like a house of cards. I told Charlotte that we could not postpone the inevitable any longer when it became apparent that we would have to declare Chapter 11 and let the 130-acre property fall into bankruptcy court.

Few marriages survive bankruptcy, but when you add fathering a child out of wedlock to the equation, it was amazing that Charlotte and I stayed married as long as we did. Once again, I found myself in divorce court, but this time there weren't as many assets to divide up. I gave Charlotte a nutritional-products business that she was running out of our home, $100,000 worth of furniture and antiques, and several years of my ATP pension plan, worth about $800 a month. All I asked for in return were my tennis trophies.

The judge, in his decree, agreed to our terms and ordered me to pay Charlotte $7,000 in monthly child support for Anne and

Tamara. I didn't see how that was possible. After I took that part-time job at Grove Isle in South Florida, I commuted back and forth to Tennessee, but after a while, my return trips became more and more infrequent. In many ways, I had abandoned the girls—physically and emotionally. For instance, I missed Tamara's birthday one year because I wanted to party with some friends in the Cayman Islands. I went for weeks without calling from Coconut Grove because I was too "busy." Unlike John McEnroe, I was no candidate for Father of the Year.

In quiet moments, I felt guilty for the way I was treating the girls, but obviously, I didn't feel guilty enough to change my behavior.

Sailing Away

While I was waiting for the divorce to Charlotte to become final, I parked myself at Grove Isle and plotted my next move. That's when I became reacquainted with a young single mom named Margaret Barna. Our paths had crossed several years earlier, and she was now living in Miami. We hooked up again, and I began spending all my free time with her. Margaret, who had blond hair and a pleasing smile, was the divorced mother of twin teenage girls. I didn't see that as an impediment to a relationship since I was a soon-to-be twice-divorced father of three—no, make that four—girls. (Like my father, I too had difficulty producing a male heir to pass along the Tanner name.)

Here we go again: love at first sight. Margaret really was the one I had to spend the rest of my life with. I couldn't let her get away, so I quit the Grove Isles job and started teaching at the Treasure Island Tennis & Yacht Club on Treasure Island, just outside of St. Petersburg. I moved into a condo with Margaret and her girls.

The west coast of Florida looked like a good place to hang my shingle. The Treasure Island Tennis & Yacht Club was an upscale club filled with active and well-heeled members. The "dot-com" economy was still roaring in 2000, and I thought there would be plenty of interest in all types of teaching programs, which is where tennis pros make their money.

This was the first time I had ever worked at a club with the word *yacht* in the title. The Treasure Island Tennis & Yacht Club sported 15 courts and a well-appointed clubhouse adjacent to a causeway where slips were decorated with Hatteras sportfishing boats and sleek Mariah cigarette-style cruisers. Yachting was definitely part of the Treasure Island lifestyle, and when the management told us that they could find us a hard-to-come-by slip, Margaret and I began talking about getting a boat. Cruising the calm waters of the placid Gulf of Mexico with friends and a margarita in hand sounded like a nice way to spend a Sunday afternoon.

In late spring 2001 we began poking around to see what was available in the used-boat market. Our inquiries led us to a boat broker named Gene Gammon. He listened to our desires and then said he had just the boat for us: a 32-foot Wellcraft that came with a well-equipped cabin and room to sleep four.

We took the boat out on a test cruise, and Margaret and I agreed that we could get used to this type of recreation. Something about the wind in our hair and salt-flavored breeze appealed to us. We caught the sea bug, and all it would cost was $39,000.

Just one little nagging problem—money. Covering the $7,000 a month I owed Charlotte in child support didn't seem possible. I was spending my lesson earnings as quickly as they came in on rent, food, and a car. What I needed was another deal, which, fortunately for me, was brewing. Three large residential builders had contacted me about providing tennis facilities in the middle of their planned developments. These tennis, fitness, and spa facilities would be called Roscoe Tanner Tennis Villages, and they would be part of residential neighborhoods in Atlanta, Knoxville, and Palm Springs. My initial consulting fee would come out to $150,000, with the promise of more to come. I hadn't seen checks with that many zeros in years, so I was thinking, *Happy days are here again.*

I outlined the scenario to Gene Gammon, the boat broker, and we came up with a deal in which I gave him a $3,500 deposit to hold the boat until the fat consulting check came my way. I remained in contact with one of the housing developers, who was based in Jacksonville, Florida, and his people told me that two banks were stepping up and financing the first Roscoe Tanner Tennis Village for $7 million. Once that happened, I would be wired my first payment of $50,000.

I called Gammon and told him the money would be here any day. "Great," he said. "When you have the funds, I can release the boat to you. All you have to do is go to my bank and deposit the money."

I asked Gammon if I could write a personal check. "Sure," he said, "but you can't have the boat until the check clears."

"I have no problem with that," I said. Even someone like me who let money slip through his fingers like rainwater understood that it wasn't a good idea to take possession of a boat until the check was made good by the bank.

A couple of days later, anticipating that $50,000 would be wired to my account at any moment, I dropped by Gammon's bank and wrote a personal check for $35,500.

"How long will it take for this check to get to my bank?" I asked the teller.

"Three or four days."

I wasn't 100 percent sure that the money from Atlanta would be there in time. "What happens if my check is no good?" I asked.

"The check will bounce, but then we will try to redeposit it, which will give you another three or four days to make it good."

That sounded fine to me. I wasn't in a rush to take possession of the boat until it was legally mine anyway.

Six days later, I received a phone call from Gammon. "Your check just cleared," he said.

"So what happens now?"

"I can give you title to the boat."

The next day, I dropped by Gammon's house, where he gave us the title and the key to the Wellcraft.

I was now the proud owner of *Nora's Cruisin'*.

Aloha Time

We parked *Nora's Cruisin'* into a slip in front of the tennis club and departed on a two-and-a-half-week trip to Hawaii. Margaret's two girls from a previous marriage, Lauren Anne and Lindsey, plus Lauren Elizabeth (my daughter from my marriage to Nancy), as well as Margaret's parents, joined us for a glamorous vacation that didn't cost us much at all. Since Margaret was still working for Continental Airlines, our plane fares were free, and our hotel rooms at the Hilton Waikoloa Village on the big island of Hawaii were comped by the management in return for my playing tennis with the manager. I asked if I could do a clinic for the hotel guests, but that never happened.

On July 9, Margaret's birthday, we had a "vow ceremony" (since we were still waiting for the judge to sign the divorce settlement) on a promontory overlooking the beach.

We had quite a honeymoon, and life looked good. One of the downsides of being a tennis pro is that you don't get vacation pay: if you're not out on the court instructing, you're not replenishing your bank accounts. While the Hawaiian airfares and hotel rooms were freebies, we dropped a few puka shells on romantic sunset dinners and Hawaiian shirts. I felt bad that I had written a rubber check to pay for our incidentals at the Hilton Waikoloa Village, but I promised the manager that he would get his money.

Things were tight when we got home, and we needed some quick cash. I made a rash decision that I regret to this day: I dropped by one of those Loan Sharks R Us types of places—the ones in strip malls that promise "payday loans" and "advance money"—to borrow some quick cash. I now had something to put up as collateral—the *Nora's Cruisin'*.

"How much do you need?" the young clerk behind the counter asked.

"Ten thousand bucks."

The paperwork was quickly drawn, and I signed page after page, but I didn't read the fine print because I expected the next $50,000 to arrive any day, and Loan Sharks R Us would get their money back.

I wish I *had* read the fine print because I had just signed a loan that would charge me 10 percent interest *per month!* I could have gotten a better deal from the Mob!

Three weeks later, I received a phone call that rocked my world. Gene Gammon was on the line.

"Roscoe, I've got some bad news. Your check bounced," he declared.

My heart skipped a beat. "Wait a minute. You told me it cleared."

"Doesn't matter. It bounced."

"What does this mean?" I asked, stalling for time while my mind scrambled to process how this was going to affect my future.

"You either need to make that check good or give me back the boat."

"Give you back the boat . . ." I said out loud, but inside, I was thinking, *I can't return the boat. I owe ten grand on it!*

"Listen," I said. "I need to make a phone call. I'll have to call you back."

Gammon told me to stay in touch, and then I hot-dialed the developer's offices in Jacksonville.

"Roscoe, I have some bad news," my contact said.

I couldn't bear more bad news on the same day. "Give it to me," I stated.

"The banks have decided to finance half of the $7 million package we asked for. That means we have to scale back on the project, so the decision has been made to drop the Roscoe Tanner tennis and fitness facilities from the site plan. Sorry about that."

He was sorry? What about me? I was left holding a large bag with a 32-foot Wellcraft cabin cruiser in it. I would have loved to hand the keys back to Gene Gammon and be rid of it, but first I had to find a way to pay back that $10,000!

The next few months were living hell for me. When I failed to make my payments with Loan Sharks R Us, they repossessed the boat. Gammon became livid when he heard that news. He thought *he* had the boat as collateral, but a loan company had beaten him to the repossession hook. Now all he had was a promissory note from me to pay $35,500.

I offered him my ATP pension plan, which was due to start paying me around $880 a month when I turned 50 in a few months. That pension plan would pay out a steady $880 a month for 20 years and eventually be worth a little more than $100,000, but Gammon wasn't interested in a long-term payment plan. He told me in no uncertain terms that he wanted to be paid in full *now*.

I felt my fortunes sinking like a boat with a gaping hole in the hull. Over the next two years, Gammon hounded me through the courts and in our personal interactions. I employed every excuse in the book to stall for time. "Once this deal goes through" was my mantra. I really believed that if I held out long enough, something good would happen or I wouldn't have to pay him somehow.

At Treasure Island, the management informed me that from now on, I couldn't charge more than $50 an hour for lessons and that I would have to give the club *half* that amount. Twenty-five dollars an hour wasn't going to cut it in west Florida—or help me pay my humongous debts.

That's when I heard there were better opportunities for senior tennis players in Europe. The ball hadn't bounced my way for a long time. Why not go for a change of scenery in a wonderful part of the world? As Margaret and I discussed our options, the fact that our daughters (I really viewed them as my flesh and blood) could experience European culture appealed to us. They could receive an education that would put them ahead of kids their age back in the United States. They could learn another language—or two—and be able to speak it fluently.

I had contacts in Europe who could help us get a fresh start. That promising British player, Simon Dawson, had contacted me about coaching him on the ATP tour. If that didn't pan out, I knew players from my old touring days who had bought clubs or were involved in various tennis endeavors. I could work for them, giving lessons and running tournaments.

The grass definitely looked greener across the Atlantic.

10

All Hot and Bothered

June 19, 2003, Karlsruhe Jail

After I zipped up my pants and flushed the toilet, I lay down on my bed. *How humiliating,* I thought. *And you'll be in the same room when your cellmate has to go number two.*

The stiflingly hot conditions were worse than playing a noon-time match at the Manker-Patten Tennis Club in mid-July. Our cell received no ventilation, and the solid steel door kept fresh air from circulating in the room. The summer of 2003 was turning out to be a scorcher: CNN International regularly led off with stories about the record-setting temperatures across the European continent. Even London was experiencing a triple-digit heat wave.

I had hoped to call Margaret today, a Thursday, but the jail's social worker had the day off since this part of Germany celebrated the Roman Catholic feast day of Corpus Christi, or *Fronleichnam,* to commemorate the institution of the Holy Eucharist. I always had trouble keeping up with German holidays because there seemed to be so many of them.

The dinner cart arrived about 5:00. I handed my plate through the door slot, and when it was returned to me, I saw a tin of sardines, six pieces of bread, and a dollop of butter and jam on the plate. My pitcher was filled with sweet tea.

I was thirsty from the overwhelming heat, so I poured some lukewarm tea into my glass and took a long swig. I immediately felt a headache come on—probably from the tons of sugar in the tea—but at least the drink had some taste. As for the sardines, I held my nose and ate them, along with two pieces of bread. My Nigerian roommate, Eddie, reminded me to save the remaining slices for breakfast because there was no bread in the morning. "We only get coffee in the morning," he said.

We spent most of the day watching my rented TV, and at least that diversion kept me from going bonkers. When there wasn't anything interesting to view, I turned off the TV and thought about the reality of my situation. No doubt about it: I was locked up in a German jail. This was not a dream and not a fire drill. As this reality settled into my consciousness, not only did I wonder how I would get through this ordeal, but I was also greatly concerned how Margaret and the girls would survive without me. They were dependent on me for putting some *lebensmittel* on the table, but I couldn't teach tennis lessons from a jail cell.

June 20, 2003, Karlsruhe Jail

I woke up on this Friday morning glad that it wasn't a holiday. Around 10:00 A.M., a social worker escorted me to a prison office, where I dialed home.

"Hi, Margaret. It's Roscoe," I began.

I heard this long silence. "Margaret, are you OK?"

"Yes—yes, we're OK," she replied in a shaky voice. I could smell the fear over the phone lines.

"How are the girls?"

"Shocked. They're coping, I guess. Listen, this has been pretty rough on everyone," she said, finding strength in her voice.

"I'm really sorry this happened," I said. I told Margaret that it was ripping me apart that I could not do anything to help my situation. "I'm in a real bind here," I grimaced.

"And so are we. How are we supposed to pay the rent and buy food with you in jail?"

"I don't know," I mumbled. "Can you come see me on Monday?"

"How would I do that?"

"I'm not sure. Here—talk to the social worker."

I handed the phone to the social worker and listened to him tell Margaret that she needed a permit to visit me, which she could pick up on Monday morning.

When the phone was returned to me, I told Margaret I loved her and then I hung up.

I resolved in my mind to tell her everything on Monday and figure out some solutions. Maybe I could write a sports column from jail. A few months earlier, the owners of *Gazzetta dello Sport*, the Italian sports newspaper, had talked to me about writing a weekly sports column on tennis. *Gazzetta dello Sport* had the largest circulation of any sports newspaper in Europe. I didn't write in Italian, of course, but the idea was that their editor would translate my ruminations on tennis into Italian. I could write my stories in jail and give them to Margaret, and she could e-mail the articles to Italy. That would get some cash flow going.

One of the things I needed to tell Margaret about was a bank account I had opened at Sparkasse, a local bank. Back in March, we needed some money, so I went in for a loan. The bank officer said they don't do formal personal loans, but I could open up an overdraft account that I could use as a loan. So I tapped into that, eventually borrowing ten thousand euros, or around $12,500.

I needed to tell her about the overdraft account in person.

June 23, 2003, Karlsruhe Jail

Monday morning I was so looking forward to seeing Margaret that I didn't notice I was eating the driest clumps of bread in the world.

At 9:00 A.M., I expectantly waited for the rustling of keys and for my cell door to spring open. When 9:30, 10:00, and 11:00 came and went, however, my hopes were dashed.

It dawned on me that Margaret wasn't coming to see me, and I knew why. She had probably gone through our mail and discovered the overdraft account. She must have been so angry that she couldn't handle seeing me or talking to me. If only I had been honest with her months ago. Now, my lying had put us in a worse mess, and I had just ruined my relationship with my best supporter. Margaret did not visit me one time while I was in jail.

My thoughts turned back to a couple of incidents leading up to my arrest. The first happened on February 12, 2003, when I showed up for my tennis lessons as usual at the Racket Center in Nüssloch. Upon my arrival, I had a message to call Jürgen Fassbender, my old friend from the tour who had found me my coaching job. "Urgent," said the message.

I didn't have a good feeling when I reached Jürgen at his tennis club in Karlsruhe.

"Listen, Roscoe, we have a problem," he began. "The police are here to see you."

The police? A cold shiver ran down my spine, and I *knew* this had something to do with the boat in Florida.

"They wish to speak with you," Jürgen said.

I could hear someone speaking German as the phone was handed over to one of the German cops.

"Ja, Mr. Tanner, zis is—" and then he said a name that I didn't catch, adding that he was with the Karlsruhe Polizei.

"Vee need to talk vid you," he said in accented English. "If you cannot come right now, ve vill come find you." It didn't sound like an idle threat.

My mind raced. Gene Gammon's long arms had finally reached me in Germany. He had not forgotten about me. I thought I could run away from my problems, but I could not hide.

"I can be there in 20 minutes," I said, and that seemed to mollify the detective.

On the drive over, I called Rainer Schubert, an attorney and teammate on my *Bundesliga* team, and described my predicament. He promised to make a phone call or two on my behalf. Within 10 minutes, he called back to say that there was an international warrant for my arrest, so it looked like the police wanted to put me in jail for extradition to the United States.

When I drove into the parking lot of Jürgen's club, I immediately saw two policemen standing beside a silver Mercedes police car. *Here we go,* I thought. *My life is ending. Margaret, the girls, my daughters in the United States, and my freedom—it will all be gone in a few minutes.*

The first thing the detectives said to me was that they had spoken with Rainer, and Rainer was talking with the prosecutor. They suggested we go inside the club and wait for his call.

When the phone rang, Rainer was on the line. "Roscoe, they are saying you have to go to jail and be extradited to the United States."

"Isn't there anything I can do?" I asked, panic rising in my throat.

"No, I'm afraid not."

My mind raced through ideas—any ideas—that could keep me from being locked up. "What if I give them my passport?" I asked. Doing this, I knew, would prove that I wasn't a flight risk and that I wouldn't be traveling far from Ettlingen.

"Could work," Rainer said. "Let me try."

Five minutes later, Rainer buzzed me back with the news that the prosecutor agreed with my idea. I was told that I would have to report to the police once a week and come to any court dates that were required. I always kept my passport with me in Germany, so I reached into my racket bag and handed it over to the detectives. In a way, I felt relieved, but at the same time, I knew I had to find a way to pay Gammon—and it better be payment in full.

Rainer later told me that the prosecutor was reluctant to put me in jail, but he didn't know how long he could stall the American authorities. The prosecutor accepted my argument that the best chance Gammon had to be paid was for me to be teaching tennis lessons and building up my name in Europe. I mentioned that an Italian management company had contacted me about the possibility of doing clinics with them at a great daily rate. A resort in the Canary Islands was interested in having me host a weeklong tennis camp. And there was that column-writing gig with *Gazzetta dello Sport* that could happen.

Over the next couple of months, whenever Rainer asked me about the money (usually because he had received inquiring phone calls from the prosecutor), I ran through the list of "possibilities" to buy time. Several times I really thought I'd get a contract offer to do clinics here or a tennis camp there, but they never came to fruition.

The weird thing is that amidst all this turmoil, I was playing great tennis. I won significant age-group tournaments in Spain, Italy, and Switzerland, which attracted some sponsor interest. Several tennis-related companies, such as Dunlop and K-Swiss, talked to me about endorsing their products, for which I would pocket some money.

Life was looking up after a rocky beginning in Europe. The kids were doing well at the Europaschule, a highly regarded international school, and they had overcome major adjustments—such as sitting in a classroom where the subject was taught in German. But I have to hand it to Margaret. She worked with the girls around the clock, fashioning flashcards with German and French words and constantly drilling them in both languages. Already, their French was excellent, and they were taking Latin in school. I was proud of their high marks in math and German history because I knew I never could have accomplished what they were doing.

Still, the tension of having to come up with the money to pay off Gammon was eating me alive. Two weeks before my arrest, I had driven to a grassy park and parked the car. *Everything* about life was bothering me. The pounding tension built up to a point where I couldn't stand it anymore. I punched my fists and pounded the steering wheel, bellowing, "God, fix this! Now!"

I don't know why I was yelling at God. I certainly hadn't been talking to him for a long, long time. But nothing was working, and I needed money to get this guy in Florida off my back.

I calmed down following that outburst, but then a weird feeling came over me—a feeling that God was going to fix my financial problems in a manner that I might not expect or necessarily like.

That's when I was arrested at home, taken to police headquarters in Karlsruhe, and imprisoned. I spent many hours lying on my bed in that jail thinking about how I had gotten myself into this mess. Here I was, Roscoe Tanner from Lookout Mountain, Tennessee, a Wimbledon finalist who battled legendary Bjorn Borg to five sets, behind bars like any common criminal. Millions had seen me play tennis in person and hundreds of millions had watched me play on TV. Now millions more were reading about my humiliating arrest.

I had certainly been humbled and cast low. Then I remembered something from my Sunday-school days at Lookout Mountain Presbyterian, the lesson about reaping what you sow. I had sown lies and deception, and now I was harvesting a bumper crop of despair and humiliation.

June 24, 2003, Karlsruhe Jail

Today was a big day—my first shower in nearly a week. But I had only the clothes that I wore *into* jail: blue jeans, a red, white, and blue K-Swiss collared tennis shirt, and K-Swiss tennis shoes. I hadn't known that the German jail didn't provide inmates with "prison blues" or an orange jumpsuit.

A German pastor knocked on the door early in the afternoon.

"I heard we had an American," he said in excellent English. "Can I be of assistance to you?"

Here was a chance to talk with someone besides my cellmate, someone who might understand what I was going through. I welcomed him inside the cell. "Have a seat," I said, pointing to the only chair.

He asked me to tell him a little about myself. I didn't say anything about being a tennis player, but I gave him the gist of what had happened in Florida, which had a direct bearing on why I was in jail right now.

He nodded sympathetically at the right moments, and I felt he cared enough to listen to me.

"Can I leave this with you?" He had been holding a leather-bound Bible. "It's in English."

"English?" I accepted the Bible and flipped it open. It felt comforting to read something in my mother tongue, although I wasn't sure how fun it would be to read the Bible. "Sure, thank you," I said.

"Please, it's yours," he replied, standing up to signal his intention to leave.

I thanked him for his time, and the friendly pastor offered to visit again. "I would welcome that," I said gratefully.

Then I had my first visitor from the outside—Rainer Schubert, whom I met in a small room near the main office. My first concern was what would happen to Margaret and the girls.

"I spoke with some of the guys on the team, and they are going to help out," he said.

Rainer appeared so calm, but my guts were churning.

"Can you get me some clothes from Margaret?" I asked. I told Rainer how I had taken my first shower only to have to put on my dirty underwear and stinky shirt and socks again.

He promised to try.

After my visit, I asked the guard if I could make a phone call to Margaret. I desperately needed to talk to her, I said.

The guard, who spoke a bit of English, apparently knew enough to tell me, "It is important to you, but not to us."

"But the judge said I could make phone calls. I have a paper from him."

"Important to you, but not to us," he repeated.

Later, Eddie told me that German law states that if you haven't been sentenced yet, then you cannot make phone calls because presumably you could influence witnesses by talking to them. I tried to explain that I wasn't charged with anything in Germany, so that law couldn't apply to me. My pleas fell on deaf ears. I was done for.

At this point, it became evident to me that the best way to get out of German jail was to be extradited to Florida, where I would appear before a judge and take my lumps. Everyone I had talked to said that if I offered a viable restitution plan in the United States, then I could be released from jail.

If only I had faced up to my responsibility before Margaret and I left Florida. But I had ignored the creditor's demands and court injunctions against me, hoping my financial difficulties would go away. Instead, they multiplied and built to a critical mass. The long arm of the law collared me in Europe.

I was fortunate to have Rainer Schubert as a friend, who was certainly going the extra mile for me. When I asked him how long extradition proceedings took between Germany and the United States, he replied that to the best of his knowledge, it would take six months to get to the U.S.A. I could cut that time in half if I had an army of lawyers working on my behalf, but since I couldn't afford a legal advocate, I was at the mercy of the German court system.

With that news, I realized that I couldn't control anything. That was very hard for someone who was used to being in control.

July 6, 2003, Karlsruhe Jail

After two and a half weeks in jail, I feared for my sanity. The feeling of being cooped up was getting to me. I had been stupid to sulk in my cell the first couple of days during the one-hour "exercise period" that began at 9:00 A.M. I soon discovered that going outside in the morning sunshine could keep me from going stir-crazy.

The recreation hour consisted of being led outside to a heavily fenced area about half the size of a . . . tennis court. There were a couple of Ping-Pong tables and nothing else. I usually jogged around the court, but since the area was so small, I felt like a rat spinning a wheel. Most prisoners were content to smoke and make small talk with each other. Others kept to themselves and read old German-language newspapers left out for the prisoners.

I noticed the conspicuous absence of Germans in this German jail. The Karlsruhe lock-up seemed to be populated almost exclusively with Turks, Croatians, Russians, and Africans. I gravitated toward those who spoke some English. Eddie introduced me to two guys from Cameroon and several fellows from Somalia and Ethiopia. I did not go out of my way to speak with anyone who looked to come from an Arab country. They were not friendly to me either, and with the war in Afghanistan still going strong, I felt the tension whenever I was in their presence. I avoided eye contact because for all I knew, they were Al-Qaeda terrorists picked up for questioning.

Throughout the prison, I saw walls splashed with anti-American graffiti. I felt like I was walking around with a bull's-eye on my back. Would someone come up behind me and slit my throat just because I was an American? In my fear and paranoia, I wondered if that was possible.

Part of me thought it would be better to make myself a moving target, so to speak, so I began jogging 45 minutes during rec hour. At least I felt better after raising my heart rate and getting some exercise. But I could tell my health was deteriorating. The food was awful, but I had gotten into the habit of saving some bread or fish so that I could eat a little at night and not be too hungry. Often, the stew or fish dip looked so unappealing that I closed my eyes and ate it. What else could I do? I was in pure survival mode.

Life in a German jail was getting to me, and I wondered when I would snap. I seriously wondered what a nervous breakdown would be like. I had never known a life without freedom: freedom of movement, freedom to associate with whom I wanted, freedom to eat when and what I wanted, freedom to bathe, freedom of privacy.

Nearly three weeks into my incarceration, I had lost hope. I was looking at *months* in this jail, and that was only the warm-up to jail time in the United States! How long would I be locked up in a Florida prison? Could I stand the boredom, interrupted by moments of paranoia, wondering if some other prisoner wanted to make a name for himself by sticking a knife into a former professional tennis player? I remembered having laughed when I heard the jokes about prisoners who had become "wives" of certain inmates, and they were brutally sodomized in the showers. That wasn't funny now.

They say that a person can live 30 days without food, three days without water, three minutes without air, and 30 seconds without hope. All I saw in my future were the suffocating four walls of a prison cell and a life of looking over my shoulder.

I was losing hope by the minute.

On this Sunday morning, I happened to be channel surfing, looking for something interesting to watch. Sunday morning was never a good time to find captivating TV programming. It was too early for any sports-related show to come on, and most movies didn't start until the afternoon. I was alone; Eddie was in the exercise yard.

I turned to Channel 31—CNBC. Maybe something had happened in the news. Instead of broadcasting the latest news cycle, CNBC was showing the *Hour of Power*, a 60-minute program hosted by Reverend Robert Schuller from the Crystal Cathedral in Southern California.

I recognized his upbeat smile, and he seemed to be having a good time. Maybe he had something interesting to say. I watched as

Reverend Schuller, dressed in gray robes with accents of black striping, delivered his sermon to the audience, and something he said that morning caught my attention. "Turn with me to Paul's letter to the Philippians, chapter 4, verse 4," he began.

I reached for the English-language Bible that the German pastor had left me. Philippians . . . Philippians . . . that was in the New Testament, if I remembered right from my old Bible-study days at Stanford, somewhere after the Gospels. After a minute or two, I found the passage. I read the passage along with Reverend Schuller:

> Rejoice in the Lord always. Rejoice, let your gentleness be evident to all! The Lord is near. Don't be anxious about anything, but in everything by prayer and petition, with thanksgiving, present your requests to the Lord. And the peace of God, which transcends all understanding, will guard your heart and your minds in Christ Jesus.

Hmm. This passage said that I shouldn't be anxious about anything, yet my anxiousness and paranoia levels were off the charts. Reading on, it said I should present all my requests to the Lord. Well, I certainly had a few, though I couldn't expect God to listen to me. I had turned my back on him for years. Why should he listen to me now? But this passage said that if I presented my requests to the Lord, then the peace of God, which transcends all understanding, would come over me.

I pondered that passage for a long moment. I knew I was tired of going through life Roscoe's way. What had that route gained me? As I looked around my bare jail cell, I had to say that going my way had gained me nothing, absolutely nothing. I had either spent, lost, or signed over all my money. But that wasn't enough. I had ripped off friends, innocent acquaintances, and creditors on two continents. I had cheated on two wives and failed miserably as a father to six daughters. When I looked at the sum of my life, it added up to a big, fat zero. I was crawling through life at rock bottom.

I felt an urge to kneel. I had known God before, but I had spent a lifetime turning my back on the Lord, doing what I wanted. I became more and more tense. My body shivered as tears welled up and began flowing down my face. I had been such a sinner, a filthy rag in a sea of white. I needed to get right with God—for my sake. I knew that I had nothing to offer him, but I knew from my old Bible-study days that he died on a cross two thousand years ago for *me*—a sinner. Jesus died a horrible death so that I could have eternal life with him. All I had to do was repent for my sins.

I leaned over my bed and clasped my hands. "Dear Lord," I began, "I've done so many wrongs that I don't know where to begin. I want you to know that I'm sorry for what my life has become. I repent of my sins and ask that you come into my life now. I want the peace that transcends all understanding. Please give me that peace because that is the only way I will make it through all of this."

I immediately felt God's sweet presence in my jail cell. I felt better. I bent over again and thanked the Lord for hearing my prayer of repentance. Then I asked that he take care of Margaret and the girls. "Please help my wife, Lord. I can't do anything. I'm totally helpless."

I stood up then and sat on my bed. I knew something special had just happened. I looked over to the TV, and the sound was muted. The Crystal Cathedral choir looked to be singing some sort of benediction.

How appropriate. What had happened was the end of an old life. I now had a new life in Christ. I didn't know what that meant, but I was eager to find out.

11

Camping Out with David

For the next few days, I got reacquainted with the Bible. The German pastor had left me a King James Version translation, so I found the stilted English and the *thee*s and *thou*s difficult to comprehend. But this old-school Bible was the only thing I had to read in English; all the newspapers, magazines, and books from the library were written in the language of Goethe. Besides, passively watching TV around the clock was like eating dessert all day: after a while, you get sick of it.

I was hungry to learn more about God, though. I started by reading the Book of Psalms in the Old Testament. This collection of songs and prayers, many written by King David three thousand years ago, expressed the heart and soul of humanity. I was moved by the way David cried out to God from the depths of his despair. He experienced what *I* was experiencing. His psalms reminded me of the power of God's everlasting love and forgiveness, and as I read how David shared his honest feelings with God, I felt myself being guided into a deeper and more genuine relationship with the Lord of the universe.

One psalm I read over and over was Psalm 31. I felt drawn to David's theme, which was that in times of stress, depending on God required complete commitment. This translation is from the New King James Version, not the King James Version that I read in Germany. The English is easier to understand in this version:

> In You, O Lord, I put my trust;
> Let me never be ashamed;
> Deliver me in Your righteousness.
> Bow down Your ear to me,
> Deliver me speedily;
> Be my rock of refuge,
> A fortress of defense to save me.
> (Psalm 31:1–2)

I certainly was up to my armpits in adversity, and I needed God to be a rock of refuge in a time of vast uncertainty for me. But first things first: I needed to put my trust in him.

As I worked my way through Psalms, I read Psalm 142, in which David talked about prison. I could identify with this one:

> Listen to my cry, for I am in desperate need; rescue me from those who pursue me, for they are too strong for me.
> Set me free from my prison, that I may praise your name.
> Then the righteous will gather about me because of your goodness to me.
> (Psalm 142:6–7)

A couple of interesting things happened over the next few days as I pleaded with God to clean up all the disease in me—inside and out. I knew my heart was afflicted with gunk from a lifetime of living for myself, but on the outside of me, I had had a nasty rash on my left hand and on both knees for the past five years. I hadn't been able to rid myself of this unsightly skin disorder.

On Tuesday, my shower day, I was washing myself with some crummy soap, not really paying attention to anything, when I looked down at my hand. Poof! My rash was gone. I bent over and regarded my knees. No rash! *Something a little strange is going on here,* I thought. But I started rejoicing and thanking God for healing me of my rash.

I experienced two intense dreams that first week of renewal. The first was part of a recurring dream—one that usually prompted me to wake up in the middle of the night in a cold sweat. In this dream, I could see inside myself, and the sight horrified me. Crawling around inside my guts were filthy maggots. But following my conversion experience, I saw considerably fewer maggots when I dreamed. I took that to be a good sign.

In another dream, I saw my mother approach me. She got right in my face and sternly said, "You take care of your kids." Then she was gone.

I felt awful. I had been so selfish, turning my back on my four daughters in the States, and I had been a poor dad to Lauren Anne and Lindsey in Germany. I hadn't been much of a father at all—a terrible parent. I made up my mind to follow Mom's orders. The first thing I had to do was get to Florida and deal with my legal issues. Then I had to clean up my act so that I could be a good parent to my children. I needed to read good books on parenting and receive counsel from Christian parenting experts like Dr. James Dobson.

This newfound resolve prompted me to write this note inside my Bible:

> Now Margaret must know all. I must pay for my mistakes. In a way, it feels good. My life will be clean again for the first time in years. I don't know right now if Margaret will have me back or not. I hope so, but if she

doesn't want to be married to me any longer, I can't do anything about that. I just know life will be good once I solve my legal problems. I love my kids and will not desert them again.

Over the next 10 months, I would read that note to myself regularly.

July 9, 2003, Karlsruhe Jail

What a horrible day. July 9 should have brought me great happiness because it was Margaret's birthday and the day we had our vow ceremony in Hawaii. I could only imagine how I had ruined it for her. I cried most of the day in my cell.

The following afternoon, Rainer came by to see me, but he did not bring any good news to lift my sad spirits. He mentioned that he had called Margaret, but she did not want to see me. Feelings of helplessness washed over me again.

I continued to devote hours to reading Scripture. Eddie and I took turns reading the Bible out loud to each other and talking about the passage. We were "iron sharpening iron," as God's Word said in Proverbs 27:17. It seemed like every page we turned to had a reminder to "wait on the Lord." Well, being locked in a jail cell 23 hours a day gives you lots of time to wait. This experience was teaching me patience in a way that I never learned on the tennis court.

July 12, 2003, Karlsruhe Jail

At rec time today, I saw some unusual activity. When I asked Eddie about it, he said that the guards were preparing the exercise area for a "jail party."

"Did you say jail party?" I asked. I half expected the guards to roll out an old hi-fi and play "Jailhouse Rock" by Elvis Presley.

"Once a year the guards have a party for the inmates," Eddie said.

"I can't wait to see this," I replied.

At lunchtime, the prisoners gathered in the exercise yard, where the guards had done it up right. They had brought in an ice-cream stand and a Formula 1 arcade game—the kind where you sit down and steer a race car on a video screen. I drank six or seven Cokes and spoon-fed myself 12 scoops of ice cream.

My social worker made the rounds. When we talked, he said he would call Margaret on my behalf since I wasn't allowed to make phone calls. "Any special message?" he asked.

The question caused a lump to rise in my throat. I yearned for Margaret and the girls. "Tell her I miss her and love her," I said.

Two days later, the social worker called the house in Ettlingen, as promised, but Margaret wasn't home. Lauren picked up the phone and relayed the distressing news: they were out of money and out of food.

My first thought was, *They're starving.* I became frantic with worry. After explaining my situation, I asked the social worker to call Rainer and tell him about the bare cupboards in our home, which he did. Rainer promised to get Margaret and the girls money to buy food.

Meanwhile, I was getting antsy to be extradited to the United States. My social worker told me to sit tight. "These things take time," he said.

I settled into a daily routine of reading my Bible and watching the Tour de France. I have to confess that I had given bike racing scant attention over the years, but watching Lance Armstrong pedal after his fifth consecutive Tour victory made for compelling television, especially when the riders hit the French Alps. The strategy—who was controlling the peloton, when to attack, and the sprint for the finish line—was something my athletic competitiveness understood and enjoyed.

Every Sunday morning, I waited for Reverend Schuller and the *Hour of Power* to come on. This was the highlight of my week. I also tried memorizing Scripture, which I found to be difficult. One verse that I could handle was Psalm 31:24, which said: "Be of good courage, and He shall strengthen your heart, all you who hope in the Lord."

July 21, 2003, Karlsruhe Jail

I had been in German jail for a month, still wearing my Wrangler blue jeans and K-Swiss tennis shirt. I washed my shirt and under-wear in the cell sink every other day, and bathed by splashing water underneath my armpits to rid myself of at least some body odor.

Although I kept shaving (the guards gave us single-edge Bic razors), I looked pretty hideous in the mirror because I had gone more than a month without a haircut. I ordered a buzz from the prison barber. With my bangs whacked off like leaves off a bush, this was the shortest my hair had been since summer brushcuts back in elementary school.

Rainer dropped by with some interesting news that he had picked up from the prosecutor. He said I would be transferred to a prison in Frankfurt in the next week or two, where U.S. marshals would pick me up for the flight to Florida. I prayed that night for God to speed things up.

July 23, 2003, Karlsruhe Jail

Hallelujah! This morning at 7:00, a guard dropped by my cell and told me to pack for the transfer to Frankfurt. Given that my belongings amounted to a few shirts, a pair of jeans, a warm-up suit (Rainer had dropped off some clothes that morning), a tooth-brush, and toothpaste, it didn't take long to pack. I left my Bible with Eddie.

At midmorning, two guards came by. I said good-bye to Eddie, and we gave each other a hug. "All the best," I said. Poor guy. He had been in this jail cell for more than a year, and it looked like he was going to be there a while.

I was escorted downstairs, where I collected the rest of my belongings: wallet, passport, cell phone, cell phone charger, and a handful of euros. The TV rental had gobbled up most of my money.

I sat in a holding cell with three other prisoners awaiting transfer. They didn't look German to me, and we could not communicate. After an hour, we were loaded onto a bus containing a special cubicle for transferring prisoners. The cubicle walls were solid metal with a tiny slit of a window that did not open.

Man, it was hot; it had to be 95 degrees that day. We were crammed into the prisoners' cubicle, and I thought I had been put into a sweatbox like the one in the film *Bridge on the River Kwai.* As the bus pulled into traffic, I waited for the air-conditioning to kick in. No luck. Then one of the prisoners lit up a cigarette, and I thought I would choke in the noxious cloud of smoke.

The guy who smoked spoke a little English. As the bus rumbled through the countryside, he said he was a burglar who had stolen more than one million euros (more than $1 million) in 10 different robberies.

"How did you get caught?" I asked.

"The girlfriend of my partner turned me in, the whore."

We continued to make small talk as the police van moved onto the highway. This burglar told me how to crack open a safe. The area around the handle was thin, he said, so one could cut through that and pull the handle off. Oh, the knowledge I was gaining in prison life.

We had to stay five hours in that hot, airless bus before we made an intermediary stop at the Mannheim jail. By then, I had a raging headache. We were supposed to eat lunch and move on, but I was too scorched by the heat to be hungry. While in the Mannheim jail, I met an American from Tampa. When I asked him how he had been picked up, he explained that he was in the horse-breeding business with his parents. One time, he accompanied several thoroughbred horses to Europe, where they would be sold. Unfortunately for him, he got caught smuggling 220 kilos of cocaine in the horse trailer. It looked like he wouldn't be using his return trip ticket anytime soon.

It took nine long, sticky hours to reach the Frankfurt jail. As I was led to my temporary cell, I clutched my stomach from the oppressive heat and lack of water. I felt sick and wanted to die. When I asked if I could make a phone call, I was told to ask the social worker in the morning. "Maybe tomorrow," they said.

I was locked in my cell for 23 hours a day, just like in Karlsruhe, but this time I was all alone—solitary confinement. The exercise yard was bigger at least, so I didn't feel like I was running in circles when I jogged around the perimeter. I had access to a few English books, including a Bible. I studied the Bible probably eight hours a day, but not in any sort of organized fashion. I just opened up the big book and started reading. It didn't take me long to find something that touched me or taught me who God was and reminded me how much he loved me. I prayed a great deal, and when I did, I felt good inside.

Besides dealing with the oppressive heat, the lackluster food, and the absence of social contact, I struggled to cope with the tedium of solitary confinement. One bright development: my request to make a phone call was granted. When I reached Margaret, though, she sounded horrible.

"I've never felt so alone," she blurted.

"I'm so sorry," I said. "I'm really sorry." I couldn't think of anything else to say. I had been such a jerk to leave her and the girls unprotected. I never thought I would be arrested, but I should have seen it coming, especially after the police visited me at Jürgen's club in February.

"Rainer dropped by," she said. "He gave me five hundred euros."

"Thank goodness." I felt humbled by his act of generosity—and shamed that I couldn't contribute anything on my behalf.

"My parents said they would help out, too."

"That's great, but I feel horrible that I can't do anything for you and the girls." Maybe when I arrived in the United States, I could seek financial help.

"Hang in there," I offered.

"I'll try."

"I love you."

"I love you, too."

For a moment, I was in heaven. She said she still loved me. Then I had to hang up, but at least I had gotten to talk to Margaret for a minute or two.

Several days later, someone in the exercise yard told me that I could get the Armed Forces Network on the radio inside my cell. (I didn't have a TV.) That helped a lot. I listened to ballgames late at night, and the familiar cadence—"Pedro Martinez, into his windup, rocks and fires"—made me homesick for America. I could practically smell the peanuts and Cracker Jack in my small cell.

When I wasn't listening to baseball at night, I turned to my Bible. I could feel God speaking to me through the words on the pages, and he seemed to be sending one message loud and clear: patience, patience, patience.

> Wait on the Lord;
> Be of good courage,
> And he shall strengthen your heart;
> Wait, I say, on the Lord!
> (Psalm 27:14)

and

> My brethren, count it all joy when you fall into various trials, knowing that the testing of your faith produces patience.
> (James 1:2–3)

Dozens of other passages urged me to be patient with my circumstances, with others, with my lot in life, just as others had before me, like Noah, who had worked decades building the ark.

One Sunday, I listened to a Bible study on the radio in which the pastor described how God had offered me a unique promise as his child. If I went to him, agreed with him that I had sinned (having chosen to go my own way instead of his way), and thanked him for forgiving my sins, I would experience his forgiveness. He didn't say that *maybe* he would forgive me. God said it was for sure.

One of the guards—I'll call him Hans-Jürg—happened to be an interesting chap. A Royal English Guard at one time, he spoke impeccable English. He offered to read the Bible with me each day, and having someone else to talk to about God was huge. We worked our way through a Bible study from the Book of Nehemiah, authored by Chuck Swindoll. The major theme was that when you have an important decision to make, large or small, you should stop, pray about it, and then let the Lord guide your decision. This was so foreign to how I had been living my life. I wasn't used to taking my time on anything, especially purchases. If I wanted something, I whipped out the cash or let the clerk swipe my credit card. My impatient behavior was what kept me in debt. For something like purchases, I should take time to listen to God, take time to pray, and take time to wait for his response.

I was tapping my fingers, though, wondering when I would be extradited to the United States. I couldn't *wait* to leave German custody and board a flight bound for America. The Royal Guards wouldn't tell me the date because of security reasons (they didn't want me to hatch an escape plan with someone on the outside). Instead, they told me to be ready to go each morning I woke up.

That wasn't helpful as the days passed by. Then on the afternoon of July 31, Hans-Jürg paid me a visit.

"So tell me. Am I going home tomorrow?" I asked.

"Roscoe, I can't tell you, but I can say this: I don't know if it's tomorrow," he said. Then he grinned and gave me a wink.

So it was tomorrow.

August 1, 2003, Frankfurt, Germany

Hans-Jürg was right: I was flying home on August 1. Well, maybe not *home* home, but at least I was returning to a culture I was familiar with. Six weeks in a German jail had not been a mountain picnic with Heidi.

Two police officers placed me in the Frankfurt polizei van for the drive to the international airport. As we pulled into the departure level, I realized that I was leaving Europe for perhaps a long time. Margaret and the girls would still be there, but I wouldn't. I reminded myself to think forward, that the best way to turn around our family situation was for me to face the music back in Florida. I had written those thoughts to Margaret, explaining I was no good to anybody until I got things cleaned up.

I was led to the police precinct at the Frankfurt Airport, which was behind an unmarked door. A police officer thoroughly scanned me with a hand wand, and then opened up my carry-on bag and took out an extra pair of shoes, which he checked. Then he sealed my bag in preparation for my flight.

Everyone at the police station acted polite and courteous to me. A female officer asked if I wanted anything.

"If possible, yes," I said. "I would like to call my family, and then I was wondering if someone could get me a Coke and a candy bar." I had in my possession a few euros that I wouldn't need in the States, and I handed them over to her. She fetched me two Cokes and five Snickers bars, and then she found a phone for me to use.

Lauren answered my call. After exchanging greetings, I asked if Margaret was there. I didn't have much time to chitchat.

"Ah . . . Mom's not here," Lauren said.

That was strange. It was only 9:00 in the morning. "What's she doing?"

"I'm not sure. She went out somewhere."

I could sense Lauren's evasiveness. In fact, I had a feeling that Margaret was standing right next to her but didn't want to talk to me.

"I have to be running along now," I said. "I miss you all very much. Love you."

"I miss you, too. Good-bye."

A pair of U.S. marshals arrived, and their presence comforted me because they *looked* like Americans.

"Where's the file on him?" one asked, jerking his head toward me.

A secretary handed him a manila folder, which he perused.

"So, you're the tennis player," he said in a cocky manner. "We're used to picking up cartel members and terrorists. Guess something different today. Says here that we're supposed to take you to Pinellas County Jail in St. Pete. So why are we bringing you back to the U.S.?"

"I wrote a bad check," I said.

"You're kidding me," the agent said, running a hand through his hair. "You mean to tell me that we're running you back to Florida because of a bad check?" His partner couldn't believe it either.

"Afraid so," I said, opening up my palms.

"OK, then answer this question. You're not going to run on us, are you?" the agent asked rhetorically.

"Listen, I'm clinging to you guys. I can't wait to get back to the United States, even if it's a jail cell. It hasn't been a stroll in the park here in Germany."

My answer satisfied the marshal. "OK," the other one said. "We won't cuff you."

Time to catch our flight. Two German police officers escorted the three of us to the United Airlines check-in counter in Terminal 1. The marshals flashed three tickets and three passports to the agent.

"You are too late to board," he said, holding up a hand.

This news prompted all sorts of protests from the marshals. The United agent explained that we had missed the final boarding call, and our confirmed seats had been given away.

Now the German police entered the fray, and I witnessed a good row played out in English and German. The local cops didn't want to be responsible for me any longer.

The United agent punched several commands into his computer. "I'm checking . . . I'm checking," he said. "Ach—nothing. Every flight is full."

"*Das ist unglaublich!*" one of the German police officers said. It was rather unbelievable. There were *no* seats available on *any* transatlantic flights to the eastern seaboard? It didn't seem possible. But after 20 minutes of tapping keys, the United Airlines agent shrugged his shoulders. He couldn't get the three of us out that day. The best he could offer was a Delta flight the next day.

This news caused all sorts of Teutonic consternation because the Germans knew something I didn't: my extradition order stated that I had to leave Germany by August 1. Now that wasn't going to happen.

The German cops argued among themselves about what to do with me. Finally, they decided to drive me back to the Frankfurt jail where I had to undergo the usual intake process all over again before I could spend the night. I imagine that created a whole load of extra paperwork.

The next morning, August 2, was like the movie *Groundhog Day*. I had done this before: the early morning drive to the Frankfurt Airport, the police escort to the airport precinct, the introduction to the U.S. marshals, and the long walk to the boarding gate. This time, however, our seats were waiting for us on the Delta nonstop to Atlanta. We boarded the flight without incident, but 30 minutes after takeoff, the pilot got on the intercom and announced, "Ladies and gentlemen, we encountered a . . . a problem on takeoff. We lost our hydraulics. Now, there's no reason for concern, but I'm afraid we have to return to Frankfurt. But before we can land, we have to dump some fuel . . ."

A groan swept through the economy-class section. All sorts of dark thoughts rumbled through my mind. *You're going back to jail . . . if the plane doesn't pancake on the runway first.*

Ten minutes before landing, the captain came on the intercom again. "Folks, we could have a rough landing, so I want you to brace yourselves," he said.

When the 767 touched down, the brakes screeched and smoke wafted past the windows. I could smell the burning rubber. It seemed like every fire engine company in Frankfurt was waiting to greet us.

All the regular passengers were allowed to exit while repairs were made, but the U.S. marshals insisted that we stay on board. No problem for me. The flight attendants had plenty of food, and I ate two meals while we waited. Airline food—always an adventure to be sure—never tasted better after a diet of fish dip and stale bread.

The U.S. marshals still couldn't believe they were involved in a case centered around a bad check. "You're boring," one teased me.

Three hours later, we were wheels up, bound for Atlanta. After being escorted through U.S. customs at Hartsfield International, the marshals and I boarded a connecting flight to my final destination: Tampa, Florida. I would be booked into Pinellas County Jail.

Two St. Petersburg cops were waiting for us at the gate. One was holding a set of handcuffs.

"Mr. Tanner . . ."

He didn't have to finish the sentence. I extended my arms, and the police officer cinched up the handcuffs. When I noticed several passengers staring at me out of the corner of my eye, a wave of humiliation swept over me.

I was OK with that, though. After six weeks in German jail, even prison in the good ol' U.S. of A. was looking like the Promised Land to me.

12

Tampa Time

August 3, 2003, Pinellas County Jail

The booking process started upon my arrival at midnight. For several hours, I shivered—the air-conditioning was on full blast—while I was fingerprinted, posed for an unsmiling mug shot, and stonily watched correctional officers inventory the few personal items in my possession. A correctional officer handed me a large-sized blue jumpsuit and asked me to hand over my stinky K-Swiss tennis shirt and blue jeans. Another layer of dignity had been stripped from me. Now I was just another prisoner with a number: #S01034635.

Sometime around 3:00 A.M., two guards accompanied me to a temporary cell that reeked of urine and body odor. At least there wasn't anti-American graffiti on the walls. By the time I laid my throbbing head down, I was bone tired after a long, long day that had begun 29 hours earlier in Frankfurt.

It turned out to be a short night. The guards startled me when they banged on my cell door at 4:00 A.M., notifying me that breakfast would be served at 4:30 A.M. In my addled state, I thought I was experiencing a bad dream, but it wasn't a delusion at all. I slapped some water on my face and looked at my bloodshot eyes in the mirror. *So this is your new reality.* Breakfast that morning was a lunch bag containing a couple of bologna sandwiches, which looked like a beggar's banquet compared to the leftover bread and rancid butter that sufficed for *Frühstück* in Germany.

A lot more than food was on my mind. Now that I was in the States, I could make phone calls, and the first person I wanted to reach was my father. After breakfast, I asked a prison officer if I could make a phone call, and he said, "Be my guest." I jumped on that. I didn't care what time it was: I dialed my father at 5:30 in the morning.

Perhaps a predawn phone call triggered Dad's 87-year-old heart to skip a beat, but I'm sure that hearing my voice nearly caused a stroke.

"Roscoe, is that you, Son?" he asked, not sure if he could believe his ears.

I began bawling. "Yes, it's me, Dad. I'm safe. I'm in Florida now," I said, as I wiped away warm tears with the back of my right arm.

"Where are you?"

"Pinellas County Jail outside of Tampa."

"We have been worried sick about you. Your sisters and I didn't know what was happening. We had no idea where you were."

"I know, Dad. I wish I could have gotten word to you, but it just wasn't possible from Germany."

I quickly brought Dad up to date on everything that had happened since the polizei had knocked on my door that fateful morning of June 18, 2003.

Dad's lawyerly mind began working early that morning. "Do you know how much your bail is?" he asked.

"Twenty-five thousand, five hundred dollars. At least that's what it said on the paperwork when they checked me into this place."

"Let me see what we can do about getting you out."

"That would be great, Dad. I don't have any . . ."

"Don't worry about it, Son. We'll get you out of there."

"I have a hearing later this morning about getting bail reduced."

"Let me know what the judge says," Dad said.

After apologizing again for the early phone call, I thanked Dad profusely before hanging up.

The bail reduction hearing was surreal. Two guards escorted me into a room with several benches, where I waited two hours until I was called to stand before a TV monitor mounted high up on a wall. A judge in black robes appeared on the screen.

"Mr. Tanner," he began, as he flipped through several pages, "I see where bail has been set at $25,500. The court agrees with that amount. Case dismissed." With that, the judge banged his gavel. The hearing was over.

Twenty-five thousand dollars didn't sound too bad. When a prisoner is given bail, he must come up with 10 percent in order to be released. I thought Dad would cover the $2,550 to get his son out of custody.

I called a local bail bondsman and gave him my dad's phone number. When the bail guy looked up my case on his computer, he relayed a piece of bad news to me. "Bail's been set at 55 grand," he said.

The news felt like a punch to the gut. Bail at $55,000? I didn't know if Dad would spring for $5,500. Throughout my life, I'd never asked him to bail me out of trouble, and five thousand bucks and change was a lot of money.

The following day, I asked to see the prosecutor, since it was his recommendation that the judge followed. When I asked him nicely why bail had been doubled, he basically said, "Tough. You're on our turf now." At the end of our meeting, I took the opportunity to sign papers requesting a public defender, as I couldn't afford to hire my own lawyer.

A guard escorted me to my cell in the minimum security wing. I knew that writing a bad check was a white-collar crime, so I figured

that guys like me were separated from the murderers, rapists, bur-
glars, and gang members. *Thank goodness,* I thought.

An hour later, a guard dropped by my cell and notified me that
I had a visitor. I wondered who wanted to see me.

The next thing I knew, a prison official in a business suit was
saying, "Mr. Tanner, you are hereby served with a court order
demanding that you appear in Superior Court in Somerset County,
New Jersey, to face charges for nonpayment of child support."

"What did you say?" *I bet this relates to Connie Romano.*

"The court order states that you owe $83,000 in child support for
Omega Romano. You are the father of Omega, are you not?"

"Something's wrong here," I said, ignoring the question. "I paid
that $83,000." The money had come from the proceeds of the sale of
my house in Lafayette, Georgia, when the bank foreclosed on me
and Charlotte.

"Says here you didn't. Doesn't matter. Either way, you will have
to appear in court in Somerset County."

"When?" I wondered.

"After your matter is cleared up here in Florida, I would
imagine."

A guard who had been watching this interchange intervened.
"Come on, Tanner. We're moving you."

"Moving me? Where?"

"To maximum security."

"Maximum security!" This wasn't right. "All I did was write a
bad check," I stammered. "I don't belong in maximum security. A
mistake's been made here."

"The law states that when another state puts a detainer on you,
you become part of maximum security."

A wave of fear came over me. Being locked up in maximum
security in a huge jail like this one—there were 3,500 inmates, I
heard—would make the Karlsruhe jail and its terrorist clientele
look like a kindergarten class. I didn't know what to do . . . or say.

Then I remembered to pray, asking the Lord to protect me. I reminded myself that he knew exactly where I was and what was happening to me.

The walk to the maximum security wing of Pinellas County Jail was like marching into Dante's Inferno. I witnessed fights in the courtyard, observed scowls on prisoners' faces, and listened to taunts from several inmates.

"Hey, Roscoe, we saw you on TV!" yelled out one gap-toothed inmate from his cell. I knew local news crews had captured my "perp walk" from the transportation van into the Pinellas County Jail. Those film clips apparently had been rebroadcast on CNN and ESPN. The last thing I wanted was any notoriety inside the jail walls. I had my mind set on maintaining as low a profile as I could, but from their hoots and hollers, I could tell what they were thinking: fresh meat.

"Where are we going?" I asked my escort.

"F wing," the guard replied.

We treaded further and further into the bowels of maximum security until we reached my "pod"—a group of four cells that opened to an indoor courtyard, or "day room." I counted six round metal tables, each with four seats, inside the courtyard. Four double cells on the perimeter housed up to six prisoners each.

The guards deposited me in cell 2, where I met my new cellmates, Vatay and J. Wes.

"So you're the tennis guy," Vatay said. "We heard 'bout you. We've seen the papers."

I shrugged my shoulders. "Yup, that's me," I said.

A big black guy from the cell next door introduced himself. "Hi, I'm J.J.," he said in a friendly manner. "Welcome." He thrust out his hand for me to shake.

"Thank you," I replied, pumping his arm.

J.J. looked to be 40 years old, fit, and well built. His shaved head gleamed in the artificial light.

"Listen," he said, "I know who you are, and I want you to know that you are not in any danger here."

Really? Did I hear that right?

"Me and my buddy Ron"—he pointed to another black man standing next to him—"do a Bible study every night. We want you to come. Nobody will bother you."

"That would be great, guys," I grinned. "When do we start?"

"Six o'clock. We go for an hour."

The Bible study turned out to be a good-sized group. I met guys from Columbia, Venezuela, and Russia, along with other Americans. One of the leaders was Vinson, who stayed in another cell. He really knew the Bible forward and backward.

Another unbelievable thing happened the next day when the prison chaplain, Lyle Corpse, paid a visit.

"I heard that you were in here, so I brought you this Bible," he said, handing me a paperback New Testament with a drawing on the cover of a hand breaking free from a wrist chain. The Bible was titled *Free on the Inside,* and it was filled with first-person stories about prisoners living behind bars and in the freedom of Christ. The translation was the New International Version, a modern English version that was much easier to comprehend than the stilted King James English. The Bible also came with small marks on the edge of the pages showing how much you had to read each day to finish the Bible in one year. I had nothing else to do, so I started reading. I received the Bible on August 13 and finished reading all 66 books of the Bible—approximately 1,300 pages—by November 6.

Chaplain Lyle offered to meet with me regularly, and I took him up on that. Then I began receiving various Bible studies in the mail from my sister Sherry. But best of all was my fellowship with J.J. and Ron, who loved the Lord and wanted to be my brother in Christ.

In the months to come, I really wondered if they were angels.

Dangers Abound

One of my cellmates, Vatay, kept a different schedule. He liked to put earphones on at night and sing along with the rap music pulsating through his ear pieces. He'd keep it up right until breakfast at 4:30. After he finished eating, he would sleep most of the day, except to eat lunch and dinner, of course. I didn't complain, no siree. If Vatay wanted to stay up all night, that was fine with me.

Another guy who liked to rap all night long was Little John, who enjoyed teasing me. He tried to teach me to rap several times, but I could never get the hang of it, which prompted howls of laughter from the guys in the pod. "Hey, Deejay," he said, using his nickname for me. "You're not a cracker, but you have no rhythm."

Daily life in maximum security took some adjusting to, and living around the clock with criminals created its own set of stresses. It seemed like the system was set up to wear you down. Several times a day, the guards banged on our cell bars with nightsticks and yelled, "Lockdown!" which meant that we had to return to our cells, shut the doors, and be counted like sheep. At least once a week we had a major shakedown. Guards would search through our belongings, looking for contraband, which ranged from saved food to extra books or magazines—basically anything that would help your day go better.

Food was a big deal. First of all, what they gave us to eat was a huge improvement over what was served in Germany, but the serving sizes were very small. Eating dinner at 4:15 P.M. meant that we were all starving after 8:00. Mealtimes were interesting: after shuffling through the tray line and receiving our small portions, we found our tables. Once we were seated, the trading began. Guys traded bread for eggs. Juice for milk. Dessert for a big bite of meat. Anything was fair game, but the guards didn't want you sneaking food back to your cell. That was a no-no in their book. I got caught several times for saving a piece of bread or a hard-boiled egg, which I ate at night to stave off hunger pains. I didn't get punished for that, but they took my food away.

Once a week we were allowed to buy foodstuffs and other items such as writing paper and T-shirts from the prison commissary. I arrived in Florida without a penny in my pocket, but Dad offered to put $30 in my account so that I could purchase toiletries and a few treats like cookies. That was nice of him.

Operationally speaking, the Pinellas County Jail was light-years away from Karlsruhe Jail. I couldn't imagine the prisoners being given their own cutlery, not after what I saw during my first week. TVs were not allowed in the jail cells, but you could watch a community TV in the day room. There was so much noise, however, you couldn't hear the television anyway. I usually went back to my cell with a splitting headache from all the commotion.

Besides college and pro football games, the most popular shows were *Cops* and *America's Most Wanted*. It seemed as though most of the *Cops* episodes were shot in Florida. The inmates loved watching that show because they could see their friends getting arrested. What really blew my mind was the night we watched *America's Most Wanted*, which described how police were on the lookout for a bank robber named Aiken, who had robbed 20 banks in Florida and shot a guard and several police officers.

The next evening, we were watching the latest installment of *Cops*, when one of the guys looked out the window toward the quad and saw guards escorting Aiken to a cell. We soon heard how the police had arrested him at a Daytona pool after his mug was broadcast on national TV. The prisoners whooped it up when they saw him being walked away in handcuffs and shackles.

The sight of women prisoners also caused the excitement level to rise. They were housed in a different wing, of course, and contact was not allowed. But some of the guys knew that the law library had a window in the door, and when it was the women's turn to use the library, the guys would jam up against the door to get a glimpse of them. They generally went nuts.

Like nearly every red-blooded male, I had heard about homosexuality inside the prison walls. The possibility of being raped by a man certainly ran through my mind, and I was petrified by the possibility of being brutally assaulted in this way. During my time in Pinellas County Jail, I met some homosexuals, but I was never approached or accosted by them or anyone else. I believe God protected me during my imprisonment in Karlsruhe, Tampa, and Somerset County, New Jersey. Not once was I threatened or asked to do something of a homosexual nature.

In the United States prisoners are not allowed to smoke, but I saw enough contraband cigarettes to stock a kiosk. Cigarettes, which were valuable barter material, were often hidden inside the hem of a T-shirt. The inmates lit the cigarettes by taking two AA batteries out of their headsets (the guards liked docile prisoners who listened to music all day) and standing them straight up next to each other. Then they placed two razor blades (taken from a Bic shaver) on the battery heads, and when the circuit was completed, sparks flew—enough fire to light a cigarette. I also saw my cellmates stick two golf pencils into an electrical outlet and generate enough spark to light a cigarette that way.

To keep the guards from smelling the smoke, the prisoners stood near the cell toilet and flushed the fixture after a few puffs, relying on the suction generated by the toilet flush to keep the smell down. Then they threw talcum powder into the air. My cellmates smoked nearly every night, knowing that if they got caught, the punishment was five days in solitary. They managed to stay one step ahead of the guards. As for me, I hadn't smoked since trying it once in third grade, so I wasn't about to start.

We were let outside one hour a day for rec time. Twenty-five-foot-high concrete walls surrounded the recreational area, so many days we never saw the sun. Inside the concrete walls was a chain-link fence that ran around the perimeter of the exercise yard. I noticed prisoners sitting on the ground with their backs against the chain-link fence. They would reach behind them and unscrew six-inch-long screws, which they would sneak back to their cells. They got away with this because the guards didn't search prisoners after the rec hour. Now the prisoners had a weapon.

Stabbings and beatings were a recurring part of prison life. One of the guys in my pod, whom we called Ghost, began arguing with a prisoner in the cell next to him after we had been locked in. "I'll get you in the morning," Ghost vowed.

Ghost stayed up and made a concoction called a whip. He took a spoonful of instant coffee, put a little bit of water on it, and kept stirring until the mixture whipped into a small froth. When he drank that supercondensed spoonful of caffeinated coffee, he was guaranteed to be wired for a long time.

Ghost plied himself with several whips after vowing to get back at the guy who mouthed off to him. When the guards delivered their wake-up call at 4:00 A.M. and unlocked the cell doors, the hopped-up Ghost sprinted next door and popped the guy's jaw, breaking it in three places.

The guards heard the screams of pain and rushed to our pod to investigate. "What happened?" they screamed to the prisoner whose mangled jaw looked to be hanging by a thread.

"Hit my head getting out of bed," he said. "Wasn't paying attention." Despite his pain, the prisoner wouldn't issue a peep of protest. In jail, there were retributions for becoming a snitch. Eventually, the guards pieced together the story, and we lost Ghost to solitary confinement.

My Hope to Get Out

Several weeks into my stay, I met my public defender, and I immediately liked his name: Michael Hope. That seemed like a good omen.

The jailhouse scuttlebutt was that public defenders, overburdened with a huge caseload, gave their clients short shrift. Prisoners with public defenders were treated like cattle: in you go, out you come. Many public defenders handled up to three hundred prisoners at one time, so the chances of them knowing *anything* about your case were rather remote. Most scanned your file two minutes before your appearance before the judge. Then there was another reality of the system: judges didn't treat prisoners with public defenders as well as those represented by private defense attorneys. Money could buy you a lot of things in life, including a faster, better shot at justice.

It was also known that having a public defender automatically doubled the time you spent in jail because it just took that much longer to get your case resolved. I immediately found out one of the reasons why. The public defender's office was only available for phone calls between 2:00 and 3:00 P.M. Can you imagine several thousand prisoners all trying to reach their public defender during that hour? No wonder the number was busy for days on end. In addition, what would take a private attorney three months to navigate through the bloated and overworked court system took a public defender six months. That was the way things worked, and there was no getting around it.

Bubba, one of the guys in my pod, offered to help me get through to my public defender. "I got the right touch. Just you wait and see," he said. I watched as he worked his magic fingers on the phone, knowing when to punch the numbers fast and when to slow down. It seemed like he could get through within five minutes every time.

When I met with Michael Hope for the first time, he rifled through my file and caught the gist of my case. "This shouldn't be much of a problem," he said. "You'll probably get probation and be put on a restitution plan. From what I see here, there really wasn't an intent to defraud. You also offered Gene Gammon a payment plan, which he refused. Judges like to see payment plans, so that's a good thing. The judge will also take into account that this is your first offense and that you have no prior record."

In late August, I was taken to a freezing cold holding room at 5:30 in the morning to await my preliminary hearing before the judge at 8:00. (The prison authorities always cranked up the air-conditioning at Pinellas County Jail. When I asked why, I was told that the cool conditions kept prisoners docile. It was so chilly in the lock-up that I constantly battled colds and a clogged-up chest.) I sat among probably two dozen inmates for assembly-line justice to be rendered. As I considered the outcome of my hearing, I figured I would receive a reduction in bail and, if things went really well, probation with restitution. In other words, freedom.

When my name was called, I walked into the courtroom, where I immediately saw a battery of cameras turn in my direction. I felt more humiliation knowing that the image of me entering a Florida prison courtroom wearing a blue jumpsuit would be broadcast around the world.

I stood next to Hope and looked up at the judge, who was fussing with his hair because of the extra cameras in the courtroom. "You wouldn't believe all the phone calls my office is receiving about you," my lawyer said. "It's a media circus out there."

The prosecutor stood up and quickly outlined the case against me. He made me look like the reincarnation of Jesse James. "Your Honor, Mr. Tanner is a thief and a crook. After he failed to pay for the boat, we couldn't find him. This man has been on the run for 26 months. He ran off to Europe and hoped this office wouldn't find him, but we did. Your Honor, this man deserves full and complete punishment for his crimes. That is why the state seeks a 10-year sentence for Mr. Tanner."

Ten years! My knees buckled when I heard that.

Hope objected. "The Florida statutes and sentencing guidelines say that Mr. Tanner is to receive probation when a restitution plan is in place," he declared.

The judge wasn't in a good mood that morning—or maybe he was playing to the cameras because he wasn't looking at the defense table or me when he spoke. Instead, he addressed his remarks to the battery of cameras pointed in his direction. "I don't care what the statutes say," he bellowed. "This court will decide the sentence. I'm going to give him two years in prison unless he can come up with half the amount owed. His father has the means to help, correct?"

All eyes turned toward me. "Your Honor, this is not my dad's problem. It's my problem. I don't see what he has to do with these proceedings." My father had raised me to be my own person on and off the tennis court, and I couldn't go running to him to pay debts that were my personal responsibility.

The judge tabled his decision and said he would get back to us.

When I returned to my cell, J.J. dropped by to ask me how things went. "Bad, very bad," I said, explaining how the prosecutor wanted to lock me up for 10 years.

"They're playing a 'boo' game with you, trying to scare you so that you'll accept something later on."

"So what do I do?"

"Just sit back and relax. Don't let them get to you. They're just trying to wear you down. It's the system, man. That's why when you *are* sentenced to prison, they treat you better. The recreation areas are better. The food is better, and there's more of it. That's because the goal is to keep the prisoner calm. But here in county jail, they want the prisoner to adopt a give-up attitude."

J.J. was talking sense. My best approach would be to sit back and relax. Then again, I didn't have many options.

The guys in my pod with whom I was becoming friendly told me that I was receiving all kinds of press coverage. *Sports Illustrated* had written a short article, and newspapers were running Associated Press accounts. Reporters, who love to speculate, were writing that I could get 20 years. Reading between the lines, I could sense their glee.

A nice distraction from my legal troubles was reestablishing contact with Lauren, my daughter from my marriage to Nancy. She was 21 years old, a junior at Vanderbilt, and so full of life. Like most young people, she had her own cell phone, and every time I called, she made time to converse with me. I learned more about Lauren and she learned more about me during my months in jail than at any other time in our history. After each emotional phone call, I thanked the Lord that she was my daughter.

I also prayed for Lauren and everyone else in my family during church services, which were held every Tuesday morning. The first time I attended, the uplifting songs and the message from a female pastor named Susan Klingmeyer, who absolutely glowed, blew me away. When we sang a haunting yet touching song called "Mary Did You Know?" ("Mary, did you know that your baby boy will one day walk on water? Mary, did you know that your baby boy will save our sons and daughters?"), I nearly lost it. At another service, she asked us to break up into groups and pray for our individual needs. I asked everyone to pray for the security of my family members. "I can't do anything for them from here," I said. "Everything is in God's hands."

Someone handed me a card with the "Miracle Prayer" printed on one side:

> Lord Jesus, I come before you, just as I am. I am sorry for my sins. I repent of my sins and ask that you forgive me. In your name, I forgive all others for what they have done against me. Lord Jesus, now and forever, I invite you into my life. Heal me, change me, strengthen me, and deliver me in body, soul, mind, and spirit.

I would carry that card everywhere and reread it often because the words meant so much to me.

Weeks Pass By

Going to church in prison and doing the Bible study with J.J., Ron, and the other guys was such a rich time of bonding. Learning what the Bible had to say about life gave me peace and contentment to deal with what was happening on the outside. I felt myself growing and feeling better about my future.

My new buddy J.J. had quite a history. He was a drug addict who had been in and out of jail for most of his life. He had prayed for God to help him break his addictions, and that's exactly what happened. I witnessed J.J. telling his story to prisoners who had been dealers or users, urging them to stop being "dope sick." J.J. turned around a lot of young lives inside Pinellas County Jail.

Meanwhile, weeks passed by without anything happening on the legal front. My public defender said the judge wanted to see a guaranteed payment plan, not some vague I-promise-to-make-payments-when-I-start-teaching-lessons-again type of plan. I told Michael Hope to offer Gene Gammon my ATP pension plan. That was guaranteed money. The first $50,000 of the pension had been earmarked for Charlotte as part of the divorce settlement, but beginning in February 2006, I could assign Gammon those payments until the $35,500, plus interest, was paid off.

Hope passed that offer to the prosecutor, who passed it along to Gammon, who said no. "I want payment in full," was his mantra. I felt that was shortsighted because if I went to jail for 10 years, then he wouldn't get *any* of his money back.

One of the guards invited prisoners to attend a class that he taught called "In and Out," which was Christian-based. I received an invitation as well. I have to say that it was pretty interesting sitting in a classroom with violent killers and several guys facing death sentences. Their attitudes amazed me. One named Juvie would tell anyone who would listen, "Look, guys, you better start thinking about Jesus and what you're going to do when you get out. When you're here, it's like making a deposit. Too many guys make the deposit, but when they get out, they come right back. Jesus doesn't want you to do that. We are called to a higher standard."

I had never seen such caring between men. Such was the bond that developed among us that there were times when I *thanked* God for bringing me to Pinellas County's F wing, where maximum security prisoners were housed. I felt peace, contentment, and joy among men society said were the lowest of the low.

One fellow inmate asked me what I was going to do once I got out. I shrugged my shoulders. "Probably teach at some club," I said.

"Why don't you open a Christian tennis academy?" he said. "That would be something different. You could get kids off the street and teach them tennis."

The idea, while simplistic, sounded interesting to me. I began mulling some concepts over in my mind.

October 2003, Pinellas County Jail

The wheels of justice, my lawyer reminded me, grind very slowly. One day, Michael Hope took a deposition of Gene Gammon.

"Why did you turn down the restitution plan?" my lawyer asked. He was referring to my offer to sign over my ATP pension plan.

Gammon listed various reasons, but it soon became apparent to my attorney that something was amiss.

"That is not what we offered," Michael said, who proceeded to outline the details of my pension.

Whether done intentionally or not, our restitution plan had been misrepresented from the Florida prosecutor to Gammon. When the boat broker realized that I was offering guaranteed money, his outlook changed.

After the deposition, Gammon met with his attorney, and they came to a decision to approve my restitution plan. Now all we had to do was get the judge to sign off.

A week later, we were to meet in the courtroom. I prayed very, very hard: *Dear Lord, please let the judge realize that this is the truth. Please don't let the prosecutor sway the judge's mind on this.*

After waiting six hours outside a courtroom one day, I was called inside. *Lord, help me to relax and get through this,* I prayed. The first thing I heard was the judge reading the riot act to the prosecutor. "Sir, I am running this courtroom, and you will sit down and be quiet until I resolve this matter," the judge ordered.

The chastened prosecutor returned to his seat. The judge looked at me. "Mr. Tanner," he began, "I understand exactly what you are offering, and I like it. If you and Mr. Gammon are in agreement with this guaranteed payment plan, then the court will approve it."

With a bang of the gavel, the judge's decision was rendered. My ATP pension would be signed over to Gammon for a maximum of 10 years, resulting in a payment of $102,000. I had the option of pre-paying before the 10 years had run their course.

So everything was fine. As soon as I let go and stopped trying to control things, God took over and got things done a lot quicker.

One down, one to go. There was still the matter in New Jersey that needed to be addressed: child support for a 10-year-old daughter I had never met.

My New Pen Pal

When I was behind bars at Pinellas County Jail, I gained a pen pal: a young girl living in Somerville, New Jersey, whose name was Omega Romano. I had asked her mother's permission to contact Omega, which was granted.

What a turn of events. For many years, I had denied being the father of the daughter who was born out of a one-night stand at the Waldorf Hotel in New York City. At the time, I believed that a messy affair and a resulting love child would tarnish my carefully cultivated reputation. If only people knew! For years, I fought Connie off in the courts until I was ordered to undergo a blood test. The results stated that I had a 99.4 percent chance of being Omega's father.

Did I do an about-face and attempt to establish a relationship with the young girl, who certainly deserved a better fate? The answer is no.

After my dream in which Mom got in my face and said, "You take care of your kids," I knew that had to change. I had to get things right with all six of my daughters, and that included an innocent girl in New Jersey.

I had known from my time in Germany that my legal woes wouldn't be over once Gene Gammon accepted a court-approved payment plan, but the situation in New Jersey baffled me. I had paid around $83,000 in child support, and I could show the court proof. So why was I being held up as a "deadbeat dad"?

I wouldn't find out until I was extradited to New Jersey.

13

In Limbo

November 19, 2003, Pinellas County Jail

After three months of doing time at Pinellas County Jail, I was looking forward to being extradited to New Jersey as much as I would have been keyed up to battle Bjorn Borg on Centre Court. A week had passed since the judge had granted me probation following his acceptance of my restitution plan. *Maybe today,* I thought.

After breakfast, I lay down on my bed and napped. A guard interrupted my reverie.

"Tanner, time to roll it up," he barked. I looked at my watch: 7:00 A.M. So today was the big day. A quick plane ride to New Jersey, and then I'd stand before a judge to deal with my child-support problem. I doubted I could hurdle all the legal issues by Thanksgiving, but Christmas in Lookout Mountain was sounding like a possibility.

J.J. and the boys helped me pack. Tension filled the air: we all knew that we might not see each other for a long, long time. We wrapped our arms around each other, and a few tears were shed.

"God be with you," said Ron.

"We'll be praying for you," J.J. chimed in.

I thanked the guys and followed the guard to the holding cell, where I saw my old clothes lying in a bundle. Talk about an emotional feeling—what was left of my worldly possessions could be held in my arms. I changed into my blue jeans and that smelly tennis shirt and waited.

A woman sergeant visited me. "I'm afraid you can't take the rest of your clothes with you," she said.

"Really?" That pile of old clothes meant something to me. This was very personal.

"Sorry. Rules, you know. We can hold your personal items until somebody comes by to pick them up, but we can only hold them for a month."

This didn't seem fair, but I wasn't in a position to argue. I was allowed, however, to keep my Bible, a Bible study that my sister had mailed to me, my toiletries, a warm-up jacket, and the clothes on my back.

I received more unpleasant news a half hour later. The transportation sergeant informed me that I would *not* be flying to New Jersey but traveling by bus.

"How long will it take?"

"Might take up to a week. I dunno," said the sergeant, clearly unconcerned. "We are not allowed to tell you the route or when you will arrive. Security reasons, you know. The law states that we have 180 days to get you there, so figure sometime between a week and six months."

Six months? Did I hear right? I had heard all sorts of horror stories about bus transfers while in Pinellas County Jail—stories about prisoners bouncing around the back of a battered inmate bus for weeks on end while the guards picked up and delivered prisoners all over the map. Think *Con Air* on the interstate.

The most humiliating aspect of the transfer process was having my hands cuffed and shackled to a metal chain that wrapped around my waist and connected to ankle restraints. I felt like I had joined a chain gang, and images of *Cool Hand Luke*, the sixties movie starring Paul Newman and George Kennedy, ran through my mind. I half expected to see pockmarked guards in wide-brim hats wearing mean scowls and mirrored sunglasses.

That wasn't quite the case, but it wasn't too far off. I, along with two other prisoners in similar restraints, was led to a white 15-passenger van whose side windows had been lined with wire mesh. We sat down on the bench seats behind a wire partition that separated us from the front passenger compartment. The guard sitting in the shotgun seat wasn't wearing mirrored shades, but he was literally riding shotgun: he made it a point to show us his double-barreled .16-gauge Remington, along with a taser gun on his hip. The message: these armaments would stop any light-footed fugitives—"runners"—in their tracks.

Our best view was peering forward through the partition or looking out the rear window. From what I could gather, it looked like we were heading east toward Tampa, not north toward New Jersey. I found out why two hours later when we stopped and picked up three more inmates. One was a young guy who had cashed fake checks. He boasted that he had defrauded suckers out of $320,000, which made my Gene Gammon boat check seem like beginner's play. And there was no intention to defraud on my part!

Another convict babbled incessantly, not making any sense. His teeth had rotted out, a sure sign of heroin abuse. He mumbled something about being 40 years old, but he looked 70 to me.

The highlight of the day was when the guards bought us McDonald's Quarter Pounders with cheese and fries for lunch. We had to stay in the van and eat, however, and the guards did not remove the handcuffs or shackles. Picture this: six convicts eating burgers and fries with our hands shackled to our waists. I felt like a Cirque du Soleil contortionist leaning over, straining to reach the juicy hamburger with my mouth. More humiliation. In some ways I felt like we were being treated like caged animals, bound and restricted as we were, but this was reality.

The first day, we visited 19 jails, loading and unloading prisoners, and we hadn't even left Florida yet. Our last stop was at 4:00 A.M. at Bradford County Jail in north Florida, where we would spend the next few days.

The Bradford jail resembled a dungeon—similar to my first lockup in Germany. The authorities used two pods for the transfer inmates and kept us in semidarkness. The filthy jail cells hadn't been cleaned since I last played Wimbledon. Because of the overcrowded conditions, soiled bunk beds lined the dirty walls of the day room. Dirty papers and food wrappers lay on a floor of chipped and cracked concrete. I noticed recluse spiders climbing out a drain and scampering into the jail cells. I was terrified of those spiders because I knew people died from their bites.

Some of the guys played cards or dominoes to pass the time, since there was no TV. I sat in on a few hands, but mostly I read my Bible, leafing through the passages of Scripture for encouragement. If I thought about my situation for any length of time, this transfer jail depressed me. My spirits were lifted, however, midway through my second morning, when a young black guy approached me.

"How ya doing?" he asked.

"Hanging in there. Yourself?"

"I saw you reading your Bible, so I figured you're a brother in the Lord."

I smiled. "It's great to meet another Christian. My name's Roscoe."

"Ward."

"What are you doing here?" I asked.

"I'm waiting to be transferred to a jail 30 minutes from here, but it's taking forever to get out of this hellhole."

"How long you been here?"

"Four days."

"It takes that long to get transferred?"

"Sometimes longer, I heard. Most of the guys have been here more than a week."

I whistled, and I'm sure I didn't look like a happy camper.

"Don't feel bad," Ward said brightly. "The Lord will protect you. He knows what's happening to you and to me. Let me encourage you to remain steadfast in your faith. God doesn't leave anything to chance, not even us meeting today."

What an encouragement Ward was! We talked for hours, and he opened his Bible to Psalms. "I'm going to give you a little homework," he announced. "I want you to read the following psalms . . ." and he proceeded to write down two dozen chapters and verses.

Soon, the guards came for Ward, and I waved good-bye. I kept his list of uplifting psalms in the front of my Bible and read them several times, followed by prayer that I, too, would leave soon.

In the Neighborhood

The guards' boisterous shouts to "roll it up" startled me because they came in the middle of the night. I had been locked up in the Bradford transfer pod for six or seven days: I had lost track. After gathering my belongings, a correctional officer handcuffed me and shackled my hands to the chain that wrapped around my waist and ankles. A half dozen prisoners and I were loaded onto an unmarked, slightly battered Bluebird prisoner bus at 3:00 A.M.

Through my window I could see that we were headed north on Interstate 75. At least we were traveling in the right direction. Just after dawn, my heart beat faster when I spotted a handsome highway sign announcing our arrival into Macon, Georgia, home-town of my sister Sherry. Then I spotted the off-ramp for Sherry's house! My heart melted for my oldest sister. She had been a huge blessing to me during my stay at Pinellas County Jail. She had mailed me a Bible study called *Breaking Away* by speaker Beth Moore, as well as encouraging notes.

We continued to make good time up I-75, not making any stops until we passed Atlanta. Happily, the bus had a bathroom on board, as well as two TVs that played movies. Then I noticed the bus turn east. When I asked why, three prisoners said they were destined for a prison in Helen, Georgia, located in the northeast corner of the state. An hour later, we left the interstate and followed a series of rural roads, slowing our progress. The driver got lost a few times and had to ask for directions.

The natives in the back were getting hungry—and restless. The driver pulled into a Hardee's for burgers and fries again, and I knew the drill: bending over to my belly button to take a bite from my shackled hands. We found the prison, dropped off three prisoners, and kept on moving.

The next morning, I awoke to new scenery: the Great Smoky Mountains. Soon we would be in the vicinity of Chattanooga and Lookout Mountain. When we passed through the heart of Chattanooga, I choked up thinking about Dad. A part of me was thankful, however, that he wasn't seeing his son handcuffed and shackled like a common criminal.

The restraints caused my hands and legs to ache, and my skin had been rubbed raw in several places. There was no use complaining because the guards had already said that they didn't care about us. So I prayed, asking God to take the pain away from me. One hand restraint became a little loose. I pulled out my right hand a little bit and felt immediate relief. I had to be careful, though, when the guard walked through the bus. I had been warned that fooling around with the hand and foot restraints would be considered an attempted escape, which would result in a beating and five more years in jail. So I had to be *very* careful.

For the next four days, I lived on that bus and subsisted on a *Super Size Me* diet. The prisoners had no say in when or where we stopped to eat, nor did the guards ask us for our orders. They usually pulled into a McDonald's and returned to the bus with bags filled with Quarter Pounders with cheese, fries, and a large Coke for each prisoner. Breakfast was an Egg McMuffin, hash browns, and orange juice—no coffee. We were limited in what we could eat anyway: it wouldn't have been possible to eat a salad or pancakes with a knife and fork, so we made do.

Wolfing down three fast-food meals a day wasn't a healthy experience at all. Like Morgan Spurlock of *Super Size Me* movie fame, I experienced significant weight gain (I added 15 pounds during the trip to New Jersey) along with headaches, depression, and mood swings—a natural consequence of not eating any fruit or vegetables.

Crossing the Mason-Dixon Line

When we swung around Nashville, I thought of my oldest daughter, Lauren, who was attending Vanderbilt. What was she doing at this moment? Was she happy? All I could do was wonder.

We headed for Kentucky to drop off a few prisoners. The next day, we veered toward North Carolina and Virginia. From Virginia, we sliced through West Virginia on Interstate 81 and headed into Pennsylvania. At least we were finally pointed toward New Jersey.

Then the bus headed west—the wrong way. The prisoners whispered among themselves about what that meant, but the last thing we could do was ask, "Are we there yet?" Nor could we whine about when we would get to our jail. Either outburst would have merited a punishment: no food and no movies.

I was counting the number of movies I had watched to this point: 26. Many were repeats. My favorite was *The Fugitive*, which seems like a strange movie to show prisoners on a transfer bus, but that's what we were shown.

The bus pulled off the freeway and drove to Perry County Jail in New Bloomfield, Pennsylvania. For the first time in 10 days, we left the bus and were processed into the jail.

How long would we be here?

I knew better than to ask, but I heard some of the prisoners saying that we would be leaving on a different bus.

The guards laid out the program. We would be locked in our cells for 22 hours a day. The other two hours were for taking showers or stretching a bit in the exercise yard. We were not allowed to touch the pay phones; doing so would be considered an attempted escape, which would add five years to our sentence.

I was partnered with a prisoner—let's call him Bill—due to be delivered 30 miles away from my final destination at Somerset County, New Jersey. Bill told me that he was anxious to clean up a 12-year-old DUI charge. As I sat in a cell with him all day long, he revealed more details. He had a violent history. The state of Florida had taken away his children. Everyone was jobbing him.

Bill seemed to be a nice guy, but listening to him harangue the cops and threaten to sue everybody who crossed his path got to me. By the third day, I thought I was losing it. To keep my sanity, I poured myself into my Bible. I read constantly, which helped me a great deal. I asked Bill if I could read the Bible out loud to him, thinking it might help address his bleak situation. Listening to spiritual matters prompted him to talk about demons and ghosts that he had seen during his life. That was spooky.

I greatly missed Margaret and the girls back in Germany, as well as my immediate family. I hoped they were OK.

One day, I asked the pod runner if he could get a book for me.

"What kind of book?" he asked.

"I don't care. Bring me a mystery or something."

When he returned with a paperback book for me, I was stunned by the title of this *New York Times* best-seller: *Omega*. That was the name of my daughter—and the reason I was being extradited to New Jersey. I felt like God was reminding me of the great things to come. Someday, I would get to meet Omega.

On my sixth day in Perry County Jail, the lights suddenly burst forth at 3:00 A.M. "Time to roll it up," a guard growled.

After gathering our belongings, we were led to a holding cell near the jail entrance. After a two-hour wait in the predawn darkness, a Bluebird transfer bus rolled up. They dropped off a few guys, including one unruly prisoner who needed to be restrained by two guards.

"Take your hands off me!" he screamed. "I killed three of you @#$% cops before, and I'll do it again. Tell me your names! I want to kill you and your families!"

The guards dragged the manacled prisoner to a nearby room and shut the door. I heard a bunch of commotion, more yelling and screaming—then suddenly nothing. Twenty minutes later, the guards led the prisoner—who was being completely cooperative now—back on the bus.

Bill, my cellmate, was chained to me for our walk to the bus; he was as eager to leave as I was. I thought it had been 12 days since I left Pinellas County Jail. Riding a prisoner bus was like entering the twilight zone, a dimension as vast as space and as timeless as infinity. We were traveling through a lost world, a forgotten people subsisting on a diet of fast food for breakfast, lunch, and dinner. A sobering thought came to my mind: *No one in the entire outside world knows where I am at this moment.*

Someone in the prison system knew where I was—or at least I hoped so. The bus motored to the Pennsylvania town where Bill was to be imprisoned. Then we drove right past his jail! Bill jumped up and down with excitement, but I held him down. "Don't ask why the bus didn't stop," I admonished. "The guards don't like to be asked questions."

We drove a mile past his jail and pulled into a McDonald's parking lot. Time for another Egg McMuffin and hash browns while wearing handcuffs and shackles. The bus turned around and dropped Bill off at the jail. My heart sank, though, when the bus headed west once again.

Two hours later, we dropped off the cop killer, which relieved me. We finally turned east—a good sign. We stopped at a small county jail to drop off four inmates, then got on the road again. After eight hours on the road, we rolled into a community center of some sort late in the afternoon.

We saw a dozen cots stacked in a corner, but we were told not to touch them. They brought us several cardboard boxes of pizza—a welcome change from cheeseburgers—to pass around. We sat cross-legged on the floor and ate.

After a few uncomfortable hours on the linoleum floor, the guards rolled in a TV to show movies. I lay down on my side and tried to watch, but I was so uncomfortable.

As the night wore on, we were given no blankets, no pillows—nothing. Even worse was the guards' attitude: total disgust with the wretched prisoners they had to watch. I curled up in a fetal position and closed my eyes, but I must confess that it was very uncomfortable lying on that slab floor, my head unable to rest on my hands since I was still handcuffed.

I woke up with a numb shoulder and a sour mood. At dawn, we stumbled back on the bus, for which my sore body was grateful.

Within an hour, we crossed into New Jersey. For most of the day, we dropped off prisoners at various jails. Late that afternoon, we rolled into another jail parking lot. I thought I had seen a sign saying "Somerset County Jail"—my new home.

"Roscoe Tanner, present yourself," a guard with a clipboard yelled out.

I thought my long ordeal would soon be over, but that didn't turn out to be the case at all.

December 3, 2003, Somerset County Jail

I don't know why, but being booked into Somerset County Jail was a breeze, and even the guards were friendly. They allowed me to call Sherry right away, and my sister, who had been wondering if I had fallen off the face of the earth, was glad to hear my voice.

After one night in isolation, I was transferred to the minimum security wing of the jail. No bars! From my bunk, I could see the courthouse through the double-pane window. My spirits lifted dramatically.

Soon I would be free, and I prayed that Margaret and the girls were OK. Sherry said that she had heard from Margaret's parents, who lived near Houston, Texas, and that they were sending their daughter money to pay the rent and buy groceries. I thanked God for their generosity.

I noticed an immediate difference in the other inmates. Everyone seemed calmer, less wary of their surroundings. On my second day in New Jersey, the guards showed the Disney film *Pirates of the Caribbean*, which had just been released on video. Watching a newly released movie was a nice surprise that I enjoyed.

I volunteered to perform some clean-up duties with a guy named Dave. We helped serve meals and clean up, and we were also responsible for cleaning the upstairs shower and toilets. Actually, I didn't mind cleaning the bathroom because I knew that at least *our* toilets would be hygienically spick-and-span. For doing this work, we would be credited "good time" and a little extra food.

I received an interesting letter a week or so after I arrived. Someone at an investment firm wrote, saying they had been looking for me for several years. Apparently, I was owed several thousand dollars after an investment had been dissolved years earlier.

I wrote back, asking them to send the check to Sherry's house. I granted my sister power of attorney, which she used to open a bank account for me. A few weeks later, she sent me a check for $200, which I used to establish an account in jail. The first thing I purchased was a pair of Nike running shoes. My K-Swiss tennis shoes, which I had been wearing on the day I was arrested in Germany, were pretty well broken in by now.

A guy named Maurice—who narrowly escaped traveling to Jonestown, Guyana, just before Jim Jones forced his flock to drink grape Kool-Aid laced with cyanide—asked if he could have them, since he didn't have any sneakers. He wanted to run with me during our rec hour, so I gladly gave him my old shoes. Maurice liked my old K-Swiss so much that he insisted I autograph them for him!

December 6, 2003, Somerset County Jail

Last night, I dreamt about Margaret. In my dream, I got mad at her, and our marriage ended. I had had variations of this dream for more than a month because I was worried whether our marriage could survive my incarceration. That morning, I prayed and asked God to lift these negative thoughts from me.

I called Dad and told him I just knew I would get out of jail any day. "I can't wait to get out of here and come down to Lookout Mountain," I bubbled.

"I sure hope so, but don't get your hopes up," he said.

I ignored Dad's wise counsel. I wanted freedom pretty bad, and I was sure that it was around the corner.

A few days later, December 9, I remembered that it was the twins' birthday, Lauren and Lindsey. I wished I could call them in Germany and wish them all the best on their 15th birthday, but that was an impossibility.

After settling into my new surroundings, I expected the legal system to catch up with me. I still hadn't heard from anyone in the public defender's office. No word on a court date, but guys in my pod told me that nothing would happen until after the New Year's holiday, for sure.

My spirits went further into the dumper when we were moved temporarily to a gymnasium while a work crew repaired the showers. We spent all day on the gym floor with a blanket and a book.

One time I got off the hardwood floor to stretch my tired legs and review what had happened with Connie Romano:

- Following our affair in the Waldorf Hotel, Connie called me several months later saying that she was pregnant with our child. I was scared and wanted the problem to go away.

- After talking with her attorney, we made an agreement in which I would pay her $500,000 in return for secrecy, no contact ever again, and no more demands for payments. At the time, I did not know that this was impossible. No one can sign away the rights of a child.
- If I failed to perform, Ms. Romano would have the right to seek child support. It turns out that I didn't have an extra half million dollars lying around, so I didn't pay. I was arrested in Naples, Florida, in 1996 for nonpayment of child support.
- I was ordered to appear in Somerset County Superior Court, where I submitted to DNA testing to determine if I was the father of the child. The results came back with a 99.4 percent degree of assurance that I was indeed the father.
- The superior court judge confirmed paternity, reduced my child support to $300 per week, and ordered me to place a lien on my home in Lafayette, Georgia. "I have no confidence that you will pay the child support, and the lien of $500,000 will at least guarantee a back-up for Ms. Romano."
- Shortly thereafter, I declared personal bankruptcy. The bankruptcy court upheld the lien as being for child support. When our home was sold at foreclosure, the proceeds of $119,000 were issued directly to Connie Romano as trustee of Omega Romano. The Georgia District Court upheld this as child support, and I assumed the court in New Jersey had credited me. Unbeknownst to me, the New Jersey court issued a warrant for my arrest for nonpayment of child support in 2003.
- Margaret and I, who married in 2000, moved to Europe a year later to find work and better opportunities. When we registered to live in Germany, local authorities ran a background check on me. They found no evidence of a criminal record and no warrant for my arrest. We received a permit to live there.

- On June 18, 2003, I was arrested and eventually extradited to Florida. On August 5, I was served papers regarding the outstanding warrant in New Jersey. My public defender, Michael Hope, contacted the New Jersey prosecutor to inform him of the bankruptcy and $119,000 payment. The prosecutor said he didn't care and that I should save my breath until I could tell it to the judge in New Jersey.

What a mess! What lay before me was a legal hell where it would be up to me to prove that the $119,000 had gone to Connie as payment for child support. After thinking through all this, I felt like I had been beat up.

I called Dad, hoping he'd boost my spirits, and he did when he said that he wanted to fly to New Jersey to see me.

The following day, I received some very good news. A social worker, Mrs. Parcells, had called the court in Georgia and learned that the Georgia District Court had called New Jersey regarding the disposition of funds, but New Jersey never answered, so Georgia went ahead and closed the case. That is why New Jersey had never heard of it. Mrs. Parcells requested and received a Disposition of Funds sheet from Georgia. Now I had my proof that Connie had been paid, and I couldn't wait to tell my father about it.

Later, I heard more good news. I had been given a date to appear in court—December 15. Dad said he would fly in to give me support. In less than 72 hours, I could be a free man.

December 15, 2003, Somerset County Courthouse

I awoke on the 15th excited about the possibility of release. I opened the Bible study that Sherry had sent me, and the entire lesson from author Beth Moore was devoted to being obedient and trusting in the Lord. I liked how Beth was transparent about her Christian walk and her various struggles. Her theme: faith in Christ is real, and it works.

I was thrown for a loop when guards escorted me to the courthouse. It turns out that Judge Armstrong, who was to hear my case, was on vacation that week. My court date had been rescheduled for the next day before Judge Coleman. I had mixed feelings when I received that news. I could have been released, but the delay gave Dad some time to talk to my public defender.

December 16, 2003, Somerset County Courthouse

At court the next day, everything went badly. Judge Coleman didn't accept anything my attorney said, so nothing was decided. Then when I returned to jail, I learned that Charlotte was behind the issuance of a new warrant from California. Now the state of California wanted to extradite me for nonpayment of child support.

My first reaction was, *Why not? This time, the bus ride out there will last two months, not two weeks.*

What a bummer! If this bit of news didn't finish my marriage to Margaret, I'm not sure what would.

Once again, I had to quiet my mind and remind myself that God loved me. He had forgiven me for the adultery and cleansed me from all my unrighteousness. He had a plan for me. It wasn't to be my plan, but I had to be fine with that.

When I saw my lawyer, he agreed to contact the authorities and offer a plea bargain to the authorities in New Jersey. Meanwhile, I received the cutest letter from Omega. I read and reread it all day. I was hoping to meet her before Christmas, which would be a wonderful present.

December 24, 2003, Somerset County Jail

For much of the day Christmas Eve, I watched grumpy guys play cards. I didn't blame them. It was my first Christmas in jail, and I hoped to never have to go through that again. A local prison ministry had done a Christmas church service for us, and a lady named Kathleen Roney had led an incredible service. Afterward, the inmates received goodie bags filled with cookies, chocolate, shampoo, deodorant, soap, and a notepad.

That night I fell asleep thinking about Margaret and the girls, who would be waking up any minute on Christmas morning in Germany. How were they celebrating *Weihnachten*? I dreamt about Tamara and Anne. They were taking a bath when they called for me. I rushed in, and they were on the bottom of the bathtub, looking as though they were holding their breath. I tried to get them to surface, but I couldn't. Then my dream ended. It was a reminder that I needed to be there for them.

Not much happened between Christmas and New Year's. I got into a routine of getting up at 6:00 A.M., washing my face, eating breakfast, and returning to my bunk to study my Bible until 8:30. Then I got some exercise by walking around the rec yard for one hour, followed by sets of push-ups. Before lunch, I would play some gin against my cellmate Rocky. Then I would lie down for 20 minutes or so before lunch was served.

Afternoons were more of the same: reading a Bible study, talking with the guys, and perhaps reading a book. I was back to serving time again, and it was best not to think when I would get out.

14

A New Start

As the festivities associated with the New Year faded away, two people from my past brightened the gray, gloomy days of a New Jersey winter.

Stan Smith, one of the stalwarts of professional tennis in the seventies and a Wimbledon and U.S. Open winner, wrote several encouraging notes to me. Then I received a surprise visitor: Jim Hiskey, a chaplain on the PGA golf tour whom I had met at Hilton Head Island, South Carolina, back in my pro days. My goodness, what a sight for sore eyes. If anyone had a right to say, "Roscoe, if you had only listened to me . . . ," it was Jim, but he was so gracious and loving. For several days during his visits, he showed me important passages in the Bible, and he counseled me on what I should do upon my release. Jim urged me to get connected with Christian believers and surround myself with other believers to ensure growth.

A freezing January passed, and my legal proceedings moved with all the speed of an alpine glacier. When nothing happened in February, I knew the Lord was teaching me patience again. Then a thought came to mind: *Roscoe, you're lucky that the Lord made you so stubborn. Your stubbornness is helping you get through all this jail time.*

One day in late February, I met a new inmate named Javier. We sat down in the day room, and his eagerness for conversation told me that he wanted to tell his story. Most new inmates were alike in that regard.

I had a Bible with me, and he expressed a curiosity about Scripture. "I'll tell you one thing, Javier," I said. "I would have never made it here without having God in my life."

I told him my story as well, including how I got on my knees in a German jail and told Christ that I was sorry for my lifetime of sin and needed to receive him into my life.

"I need Christ, too," Javier said.

"That's great to hear," I said. I explained the Gospel to him, and then I asked Javier if we could pray. After he said yes, the two of us bowed our heads while I led us in a prayer asking the Lord to touch Javier's life, make his presence known in this jail, and protect Javier's family on the outside.

I met with prisoners like Javier probably a dozen times during my stay in New Jersey. The thought occurred to me that God was using me inside the jail to reach others with his love. I often shared John 3:16, the verse describing how God so loved the world that he sent his only begotten son, and whoever believed in him would not perish but have eternal life.

One day after Javier and I met, the mail arrived with a letter from Connie's lawyer requesting a meeting to resolve things. This sounded like a breakthrough. Ever since I had arrived in New Jersey nearly three months earlier, I had been stymied by the "system."

It was taking time to untangle all the threads. What happened behind the scenes was that the prosecutor had interviewed Connie, who admitted receiving $119,000. From that amount, she paid her attorney $29,000, which was not where child support was supposed to go. The prosecutor informed her that she could not take that money and ask for more; to do so would be "double-dipping."

Meanwhile, Jim Hiskey stayed in contact after his departure. In one phone call, Jim suggested that I stay with him at his home in

Annapolis, Maryland, for several weeks following my release, using the time to study my Bible and plan my future. His idea excited me. For the first time since probably high school, I was doing things the right way—not Roscoe's way.

I still didn't know if I would be extradited to California to face charges for child-support issues relating to Charlotte.

It would take me a whole other chapter to catalog why it took so many months to get released from jail. Every time I had a court date in January, February, and March, my hearing was postponed. I knew that the judicial system was tilted against the accused sitting in jail. Prosecutors want to make it difficult so that once you get your day in court—finally, months and months later—you'll accept pretty much anything they offer.

I wasn't holding out at all, but I didn't want to settle on the prosecutor's terms because I didn't *have* any more money. At the end of March, I learned that the prosecutor had sent an important motion to my address in Germany, which assured that I would never see it. Why would he send my mail to Germany when he knew I was locked up a few blocks from him? My public defender, Bob Gaynor, needed to see these motions to know what the judge would be ruling on. What was the prosecutor's motive for keeping me in the dark? I could only conclude that he was orchestrating a different outcome from the one I hoped for.

Fortunately, my faith in God continued to grow. I had never studied or read the Bible so much in my life. There was so much that I had never understood or had just passed over. The benefits of receiving Jesus as my Lord and Savior had completely changed my outlook on life. I knew my time was coming and that I could do everything through him who gave me strength. I wasn't perfect, but no one is before God.

On the night of April 7, I couldn't sleep at all. I tossed and turned in my bunk because something inside was bothering me and wouldn't go away. I knew what it was. I had some decisions to make. I believed that God wasn't solving my case until I realized that I had been a rotten father to Omega. Sure, I had paid some child support, but morally I stunk. From God's point of view, I was guilty in this case.

I decided it was time to reorganize my strategy. That day, I met with Bob Gaynor and said I would plead guilty if they sentenced me to time served and allowed a civil court to decide the vexing money issues. In my situation, a civil court was where monetary decisions should be made.

Bob met with the judge and the prosecutor to present my idea, and when he returned, he told me that the weirdest thing had just happened. The judge kept saying that my case was a moral issue, and that morally I was guilty, but he couldn't figure out what to do. The meeting broke up, but later that day, the judge sent his assistant to inform Bob that the judge would accept an offer for time served and let a civil court decide the money issues.

"This is a highly unusual action for a judge to take in a case like this," my public defender said. "Normally, judges don't relinquish control of anything."

I was ecstatic, of course, but I knew why the logjam had broken. "Bob, I prayed for this result, and I knew it was going to happen," I said.

My legal counsel looked to be in a state of shock.

A day or so later, he had more good news for me. Bob had been in contact with the authorities in California, and he said they were willing to lift my extradition warrant if I would appear in a California court to answer the charges. I saw this as more evidence of God's hand at work.

April 19 was the date set aside by the Somerset County Superior Court to decide the resolution of my case. I was sure it wouldn't be postponed any longer.

When the judge walked into the chamber, my heart skipped a beat. I had never been this nervous against Borg or Connors, even though at the time I thought Wimbledon matches were a matter of life and death. How wrong I had been. "Good morning," the judge said cheerfully. "Is everyone ready?"

Just as I hoped, there would be no postponement today. The court proceeding took most of the day as the judge reviewed my payment history and the terms of my child-support settlement.

Late in the afternoon, the judge announced that he would render his decision following a short recess. I held my breath and prayed. When he returned he ruled in my favor on nearly every count. Then he turned toward the bailiff and made this startling statement: "I want Mr. Tanner out of jail in 10 minutes."

Now it was my turn to be in shock. So it really was going to happen today.

I felt like I had won the U.S. Open. I was led back to my cell to collect my belongings, where Javier was waiting for me. "Don't forget him," he said, referring to Jesus.

"I won't, Javie," I promised as I gave him a big hug. "I won't."

One of the prison chaplains, Kathleen Roney, was waiting for me at the office. I was handed a bag of clothes, my wallet, and what little money I had left. She had gotten me a room at the Red Bull Inn, which sounded like the Ritz-Carlton to me.

Father David, who worked with Kathleen, drove me there. I checked in and noticed a Fuddruckers across the street. That looked like a great place to eat. I ordered a Southwestern Burger and ate so much that my stomach hurt.

That night when I returned to my room at the Red Bull Inn, I had never felt so clean . . . or had such a desire to thank God. When I woke up the next morning, I reached for my Bible and turned to Esther 4:14, which said, "For if you remain silent at this time, relief and deliverance for the Jews will arise from another place, but you and your father's family will perish. And who knows but that you have come to royal position for such a time as this?"

I'll tell you this: I wanted to shout from the rooftops what the Lord had done for me.

15

Life on the Outside

After a fitful night of sleep, Kathleen Roney picked me up in the morning and drove me to the local courthouse, where I had to sign some papers. All routine. Then I walked over to the Somerville train station, where I caught a midday train to Newark. My plan was to take a night train to Atlanta, where my sister Sherry and her husband, Ramsey, would be waiting for me. I had called them the night before, and I don't know who was more excited about the reunion, them or me.

A 12-hour train ride to Atlanta certainly gave me time to reflect on the events of the last 10 months. I was a free man once again, but not free to do as I pleased. There were things I needed to accomplish, including getting on a good footing with Margaret and the girls.

I had no idea what the future held for me and my wife. I had written her often from my jail cell, but I had never received a reply. How were she and the girls holding up in Germany? Had she gotten some sort of job? Were her parents able to send them enough money to pay the rent and keep food on the table?

I didn't know why Margaret wasn't writing back. I figured that she felt betrayed, abandoned, and neglected. Maybe she was deciding whether our marriage had a future. Maybe she had decided that our marriage *didn't* have a future. I didn't know.

All I knew—or could control—was what happened today. As for the future, that was in God's hands. I decided that when I got to a computer, I would e-mail Margaret the good news that I had been released from jail. Perhaps then she would contact me.

Finding Sherry and Ramsey at the Atlanta train station was a wonderful experience. Their love was unconditional, and I needed that. We drove to their home in Macon, where I relaxed for a few days and ate some of Sherry's great home-cooked meals. The first thing on my to-do list was traveling to Florida to register for probation. After talking to Dad on the phone following my release, he offered to drive me to St. Petersburg.

Dad drove from Lookout Mountain to Macon, Georgia, where he spent the night with us before we headed off the next morning for the Tampa area. It was nice to spend some quality time with Dad. As the miles passed by, he gave me some fatherly advice. "Roscoe, you have a chance to start over," he said. "Take that chance. You can rebuild, but it's going to take time."

I'm sure that some people reading this book are wondering why my father didn't bail me out of jail after I arrived in Pinellas County. Whether it was $2,500 or $25,000, my father certainly had the financial resources to get me out, but he chose not to do that.

Although it was painful to be locked up in a jail cell, Dad, in his wisdom, knew that I needed to be held accountable for my actions. I did not ask my father to bail me out, nor did he offer. Looking back, I can see this was for my good. The Lord knew I needed more than four months in jail to learn the lessons I needed to learn. I used that extra half of a year to study the Bible, read excellent Bible studies, and be discipled by men more mature in their faith than I was.

After registering for probation in Florida, we spent the night in St. Pete before driving back to Macon the next day. Then I had to fly to California to address the legal issues revolving around child support from my marriage to Charlotte. This was the one last legal hurdle that I hadn't been able to resolve before I was released from jail in New Jersey.

While I was in Southern California in early May 2004, I stayed a few days in San Diego with an old Stanford teammate, Chico Hagey. One Saturday afternoon, we dropped by the La Jolla Beach and Tennis Club to hit a few balls. I didn't have a racket, and my tennis outfit was a T-shirt and some baggy shorts. I was wearing the sneakers I had purchased in prison, and I was carrying a good-sized tire around my waist.

I huffed and puffed from the exertion of hitting balls, something I hadn't done in nearly a year—and something that used to be as natural as brushing my teeth. This had been my longest break from tennis since . . . kindergarten? I was pleased that my strokes were still there, but I realized I was woefully out of shape.

I told Chico that I had kept a diary in prison and had taken a stab at putting my story down on paper. Did he know an author who could help me?

"I only know one author personally," Chico said. "I went to La Jolla High with Mike Yorkey, who has written a bunch of books, including the autobiography of tennis star Michael Chang." Chico called Mike on my behalf, and the three of us met. I could tell they were engrossed by my adventures, and Mike said my story sure sounded like a book to him. We began collaborating on this book throughout the last half of 2004.

Meanwhile, I needed to find a job. I knew that I could get a teaching position as an assistant tennis pro just about anywhere in the country. I wasn't looking for a gold-plated head pro position; I just wanted to get back on the court and earn some money teaching tennis. During my trip out West, Chico and Robbie Kreiss, a stand-out player and friend who played for UCLA when I was at Stanford, put me in touch with an attorney named Robert Johnson.

Through Robert, I was introduced to Cecil Spearman, who owned three tennis clubs in Orange County. After hearing my story and my desire to take each day one at a time, Cecil offered me a wonderful teaching position where I could give lessons at Laguna Niguel Racquet Club, Monarch Beach Tennis Club, and the Racquet Club of Irvine.

I thought long and hard—and prayed, too—about where the Lord wanted me to relocate. There was another consideration I needed to factor in, and that was the fact that my two ex-wives now lived in the Orange County area. Although I recognized the challenges of living near them, I also saw this as an opportunity to reestablish contact with three of my children, as my mother had admonished me to do in that dream. Lauren, my daughter from my marriage to Nancy, was attending school in Nashville, but she would be home during the summer and for holidays. As for Tamara and Anne, my daughters from my marriage to Charlotte, I needed to take those first tentative steps toward reconciliation.

I accepted Mr. Spearman's kind offer and began teaching in July. It felt very good to get back on the court with a cart full of balls and an eager attitude to give a good lesson. Teaching tennis all day long can wear you out, however, especially when the weather's warm. It was a mental challenge, too, hitting tennis balls back and forth with players just learning the game. I called Jim Hiskey, the PGA chaplain, after a long day on the court, and he gave me some great advice: "When you teach a lesson, teach it for the Lord." He based this advice on Colossians 3:23, which says, "Whatever you do, work at it with all your heart, as working for the Lord, not for others."

Two events happened in the fall of 2004 that I believe bode well for the future. The first—and best—was receiving a phone call from Margaret. She was calling from her parents' home outside Houston, Texas, where she was staying with Lauren and Lindsey. I wasn't aware that she was back in the United States, since we had been communicating via e-mail. I believe that Margaret did not tell me she was back in the States because I had disappointed and hurt her so deeply, and she couldn't be sure I was a changed man. As we began a dialogue through the exchange of e-mails, she must have sensed that I wasn't like the old Roscoe.

On the day Margaret called me out of the blue, she expressed her desire to reunite and move to Orange County with the girls. I nearly performed somersaults when she relayed that news. They arrived in early October, and within short order, we enrolled the girls at a local high school and found a cute three-bedroom house to rent. We have begun the long process of rebuilding our marriage, taking things one day at a time.

I knew I could not do this alone and that I needed help. That's why when Jim Hiskey offered to gather a group of men who could act as an accountability group, I leaped at the opportunity. Shortly after Margaret and the girls arrived in Southern California, I met with nearly a dozen men, some of whom had flown in from the East Coast. I agreed that these men could hold me accountable for my actions and offer me guidance regarding my finances, because they genuinely cared for me. For instance, we decided that I should not have any credit cards and that I should learn to pay for everything with cash or check. Their counsel was not to buy anything that would add to my indebtedness.

Most men have very few friends to whom they feel they can reveal anything. I believe that with this accountability group I can build a spiritual firewall between me and the temptations that will come my way. I also gave this men's group permission to ask me the tough questions:

- "Are you reading your Bible regularly?"
- "How are you spending your free time?"
- "How is it *really* going with your wife?"
- "How are you spending your money?"
- "How is your relationship with your daughters?"

Those joining my men's accountability group were Stan Smith, a former tennis champion and a mature Christian; Jim Stump, my spiritual mentor at Stanford; Tim Timmons, pastor of New Community Church in Irvine; Milt Richards, an Australian transplant living in San Diego who mentors business and political leaders; John Block, a former NBA basketball player who was heading up the Lord's Gym ministry in a San Diego urban neighborhood; Jim Hiskey, who offered to coordinate the accountability group; Colin Magliolo, an assistant to Jim; and John Devlin, a local mortgage broker who has become a real brother in the Lord.

These men have been a godsend to me. No longer am I relying solely on myself. Now I rely on the advice of men with greater spiritual depth than I have, and that's been for the good.

Match Point

As I think about the future and God's plans for me and my family, I can see clearly why I needed to go through all that jail time. I had to be hit over the head by the Lord. I had to stop and realize how I was destroying my life and the lives of people who loved me.

I take full responsibility for my actions. I cheated on Nancy and Charlotte and caused them indescribable heartaches. I abandoned children who were depending on me to be there for them—particularly Lauren, Tamara, and Anne. I was a horrible role model for Lauren and Lindsey and have been AWOL with regard to Omega. I was a flop of a husband to Margaret. I financially stiffed people on two continents.

In many ways, I identify with the story Jesus told in Luke 15 about the Prodigal Son. In that parable, Jesus described how a man had two sons. When the younger son told his father that he wanted his share of the estate now, instead of waiting until his father died, the father agreed to divide his wealth between the two sons.

You may remember what happened next: the young son zipped out of town with a full purse and wasted all his money on parties and prostitutes. Then a great famine came over the land, and the penniless son began to starve. He persuaded a local farmer to hire him to feed his pigs. The young man was so hungry that even the swill fed to the pigs looked good to him.

One day, no doubt after being knee-deep in muck and pig manure, the prodigal son came to his senses. Heck, at his father's ranch even the hired help had enough to eat. He decided to go home to his father and say, "Father, I have sinned against you. Please take me on as your hired hand."

He began the long walk back home. The father saw him from a good distance away, and he was filled with such joy that he broke into a run to embrace and kiss his long-lost son.

His son said, "Father, I am not worthy to be called your son."

The father would have none of it. He ordered that the finest robe in the house be brought out and put on his son and a fattened calf be slaughtered for a huge feast. "We must celebrate, for this son was dead and has returned to life. He was lost and now is found," said the father.

I am a prodigal son. At one time, the world was my oyster. I became wealthy by playing a game that I loved. I received accolades and deferential treatment, ate at the finest restaurants, and traveled in style. I clinked champagne flutes with Prince Rainier in Monaco, played in a celebrity basketball tournament with Michael Jordan, and grinned my way through hit-and-giggle doubles on the White House tennis court, followed by an informal dinner with President Reagan and his wife, Nancy. Even though I rubbed shoulders with the rich, powerful, and famous, that was all temporary stuff. What should have mattered was my relationships with my family and those closest to me, but I didn't keep my eye on the ball. Instead, I ran off and did my own thing until suddenly one morning, I found myself in the pigsty of life—jail—and became the object of ridicule.

Even though I messed up as big as you can mess up, when I made a decision to walk back to Jesus Christ, he greeted me like the

Prodigal Son. He told others that I was once lost but now I was found. He welcomed me back into his family and forgave me for all my sins.

I know what you may be thinking: *This has been a nice story, Roscoe, but your jailhouse conversion sounds a little too convenient to me.*

There's a reason many prisoners turn to God. When you're behind bars, when all your freedoms have been stripped away, and when you're suffering deprivation, your eyes are opened.

I had been blind before I was imprisoned in Germany, but after 10 days of introspection, of *really* thinking about *why* I was in this tough spot, it was like the scales were taken off. I was a lowly sinner, someone who had broken the law, abused relationships, and hurt those closest to me. I got what I deserved, all right. I was brought down low, and it became very apparent to me that God had delivered me to my jailers to give me a wake-up call.

I did things Roscoe's way for more than 50 years. Now I'm going to do things God's way.

It won't be easy. Although I'm forgiven, there are still consequences to my actions that I will be paying for, one way or another, for many years to come.

But now I have a path I can follow.

I don't care how long I have to stay on the straight and narrow because I know I'm not walking alone.

The cliché is that I went from the penthouse to the outhouse, from a jet-setting life in luxury hotels and the nicest restaurants to a jail cell with a bunk bed and a stainless steel toilet. But that's not the whole story. Just when I thought I was history, I found out God was just starting to use me.

This time I hear a different voice saying, "Tanner to serve."

And I'm not going to double-fault.

Index